Sunset Guide to
ORGANIC
GARDENING

By the Editors of *Sunset Books* and *Sunset Magazine*

LANE BOOKS · MENLO PARK, CALIFORNIA

Acknowledgments

Special recognition is due to the following people for providing special assistance during the many months this book was being researched and written:

Joseph F. Williamson, Garden Editor of *Sunset Magazine,* worked closely with the editors of Sunset Books on all of the subject matter.

Alan Chadwick, director of a special organic gardening project at the University of California at Santa Cruz, offered us his knowledge from years of experience in diverse parts of the world. Steven Kaffka, student leader of the project, also served as a reliable and enthusiastic advisor.

Cristine Russell compiled endless amounts of research material and assisted throughout the editorial process.

Fred H. Petersen of the Soil and Plant Laboratory, Inc. checked the technical and scientific correctness of the soils and nutrients text.

Edited by Philip Edinger

Illustrations: Susan S. Lampton

Cover: To represent the spirit of organic gardening —plants growing in harmony with nature—is a gloriosa daisy variety 'Irish Eyes' being visited by a friendly honey bee. See page 54 for information about bees. Photograph by Darrow M. Watt.

Executive Editor, Sunset Books: David E. Clark

Eighth Printing January 1975

Copyright © Lane Magazine & Book Company, Menlo Park, California
First Edition 1971. World rights reserved.

Contents

What is Organic Gardening?

The words "organic gardening," and related terminology such as "organically grown," are heard quite frequently these days. To many gardeners (and perhaps to the great majority of non-gardeners) these words suggest a different kind of gardening, a thoroughly new and slightly mysterious form of plant husbandry.

Actually, "organic gardening" is simply an all-encompassing term for some basic gardening procedures that have been followed since plants were first cultivated. *Sunset* Magazine and Books were publishing such organic procedures as composting more than 30 years ago. Nearly every home gardener has gardened organically in one way or another without being particularly conscious of it. Ask yourself these questions:

- Have you ever dug some manure into a garden bed?
- When making a planting mix, do you include peat moss? Ground bark? Leaf mold?
- Have you used bone meal as a fertilizer?
- Do you sometimes squirt aphids or other insects off a plant with a garden hose?

If the answer to any of the above questions is yes, then consider yourself as having practiced organic gardening—to some small degree, at least.

The distinguishing feature of organic gardening is that it utilizes only organic (naturally-occurring) materials for all phases of the growing operation—from improving the soil, to fertilizing, to helping a plant ward off an insect or disease problem. These practices have their roots in the cycle of nature where, in the wild state, an organism (plant or animal) is born, lives, dies, and then returns to the earth where it decomposes and enriches the soil for the growth of new organisms.

Organic gardening as a recognized practice had its first serious beginnings in Europe many years ago, but it was not until the 1940's that it first came strongly on the scene in the United States. A pioneering Pennsylvanian, Jerome I. Rodale, led a small but dedicated group of enthusiasts, many of them gardeners and farmers who ruled out completely the possibility of using non-organic sprays and fertilizers under any circumstances. All of them took more than usual pride in the size and quality of the vegetables, fruits, and flowers they produced.

Today, organic gardening is coming on strongly again, this time with an impact on a much broader front because of greatly increased public awareness of environmental problems. Its followers have expanded to include not only the all-out practitioner but the individual who sees it as a way he can practice conservation in his own garden—to whatever degree he wishes, and in terms of his own controllable surroundings.

In researching and writing this book, we have stressed the how-to-do-it aspects of organic gardening, while also trying to boil down the many technical aspects to fundamentals and to everyday language. To those who decide they want to pursue a more organic approach to gardening, we say: Expect more chewed leaves, perhaps more flies (especially if you have a compost pile), and a little more physical exertion than you were used to before. If the thought of any of these probabilities doesn't bother you, chances are that you will soon be learning many pleasant things about your garden that had heretofore been taken for granted.

SWEET PEAS, planted in winter as part of University of California, Santa Cruz, organic garden project, produced this lavish display the next spring. Highly-publicized project was conceived to impart gardening (rather than agricultural) knowledge to students. Starting with raw land, students in two years developed a thriving garden which produced quantities of cut flowers (up to 10,000 daily, in season) for the university community, plus various vegetables for the cafeterias.

Improving Your Soil
with Organic Matter

If you take a few minutes to understand the fundamental reasons for good soil preparation before going out to plant your garden, you can avoid many potential headaches. A good knowledge of "why" may then be combined with the mechanics of "how," meaning the difference between possibly harming the soil or producing a rich, fertile growth medium.

Throughout the world, soil is basically an accumulation of particles which have resulted from the action of weather on rocks. However, these "dirt" particles alone will not support plant growth. "Dirt" becomes *good* soil only when these other components are present:

1) Organic matter,
2) Living organisms,
3) Soil "atmosphere",
4) Moisture,
5) Nutrients for plant and microorganism growth.

Of great importance is the organic matter—remains of plants and animals. Whether your garden soil is easy to work, able to retain moisture without becoming waterlogged, whether it is abundant in soil nutrients, and porous enough to allow easy circulation of air depends to a surprising degree upon the amount of organic matter present.

An increase of organic matter in the soil may not only improve its physical character but may also promote increased biological activity which enhances soil fertility. The composition of the organic matter also changes, eventually becoming a sticky, dark-brown substance called *humus*.

THREE BASIC SOIL TYPES

Clay soil is composed of particles small enough to be invisible to the naked eye. In fact, roughly 100 of them would fit into the period at the end of this sentence. Because of their fine texture, clay particles tend to fit very tightly together. In the rainy season, clay takes in water slowly, often resulting in surface runoff and erosion. Once water is absorbed, it is held so tightly to the clay particles that drainage is exasperatingly slow and aeration is limited. When dry, clay is nearly impermeable to water or air, hardening to a thick crust. Plant roots have a difficult time penetrating very far in this type of compact soil, and will not grow where oxygen is inadequate, despite the fact that individual clay particles are well supplied with nutrients essential for plant growth. Because clay is difficult to till, farmers have traditionally termed it "heavy soil".

Sand, the lighter soil, is composed of particles more than 25 times the size of the largest clay particles. Soil which is abundant in sand particles is easily tilled because the large, irregularly-shaped grains fit together so poorly. This allows free air movement through the soil but, unfortunately, it also permits water to move freely through the sand, leaching out valuable nutrients as it seeps down to levels beyond reach of plant roots.

Few soils are either 100 per cent sand or 100 per cent clay.

Loam is the ideal soil, containing a near-even balance of different sizes of particles as well as a good supply of humus. The individual mineral grains in loam have been built up, through the years, into a pattern or structure by the combined action of root growth, insects, worms, and humus. The excellent granular structure allows excess water to drain away while retaining enough water for plant growth. It allows free circulation of soil air and provides easy-to-travel thoroughfares for roots. Few gardeners are blessed with a naturally loamy soil; for ways to improve a non-loamy soil, see below.

CLAY drains slowly

HOW TO IMPROVE SOIL STRUCTURE

Unfortunately, you can't build loam by simply mixing the component parts. However, if you have a non-loam soil you can improve its drainage while at the same time improving air circulation by adding organic matter such as compost, ground bark, sawdust, leaf mold, manure, and peat moss; the goal—a crumbly, granular soil.

Two mineral compounds—gypsum and lime—can improve aeration and drainage of clay soils. Each contains calcium which causes clay particles to group together, forming soil "crumbs" larger than the individual particles. That makes the air spaces between crumbs bigger, too. Do not use gypsum and lime as substitutes for organic materials, because they do not directly aid soil microorganisms, nor do they contribute to nutrient retention.

SAND drains too rapidly.

Use gypsum if your clay soil is highly alkaline because of excess sodium. Spread the gypsum on top of the soil (the usual recommendation is "like a light snow") and spade it in. This will be approximately 35-50 pounds per 1,000 square feet.

If high acidity of clay soil is a problem, add lime. First, be sure to test your soil to determine its *p*H (see page 18). Your county agricultural extension service will then be able to recommend the quantity of lime to add to your soil for the plants you plan to grow.

A large amount of clay particles in a soil means limited air space. The tiny clay particles lump together, holding tightly to water, and little space is left for air to enter. Spading decaying organic matter into this heavy soil "lightens" it in two ways: The coarse organic particles act as temporary wedges between compacted soil particles; the very fine, more fully decomposed parts of the organic matter (humus) are sticky and act as a glue to aggregate or hold the fine clay particles together in small crumbs. This loosens up the clay and allows it to "breathe".

Sandy soils have the opposite problem from clay soils—there is too *much*

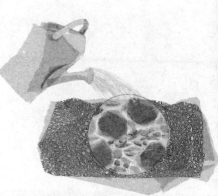

LOAM drains best.

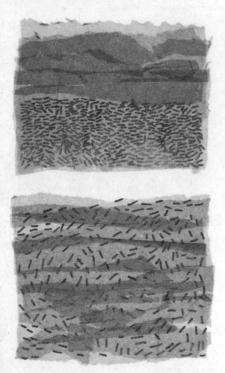

space around the large irregular particles. This lets in plenty of air but fails to hold water. Add a fine textured organic material to sandy soil and the particles will lodge in the large spaces between the sand grains, acting as sponges to catch the water and keep it within the reach of roots.

Soil fertility. Many of the valuable soil nutrients necessary for plant growth are held in the water films which surround each soil particle. The nutrients are held in solution from which they are taken in by the plant roots.

It is a general rule that the finer the texture of a soil, the more nutrients are available: As explained in the previous section, the fine clay particles provide more "clinging" surfaces, in a given space, for the attachment of water and nutrients; sandy soils do not hold tightly to water, and nutrients are easily leached away. The addition of organic matter to clay soil helps in this way: Clay becomes aggregated and roots can more easily penetrate the soil to come in contact with the nutrient supply. Added to sandy soils, organic matter holds water and nutrients in the upper soil level where roots will have access to them.

Soil temperature affects timing of plant growth and often determines survival. When spring temperatures begin to rise, it is the sandy, coarse-textured soils which warm up first. This early warmth means earlier growth of a vegetable or flower garden. It is the large pore spaces and good aeration of the light sandy soils which favor an equilibrium between soil temperature and the atmosphere.

In contrast, the heavy clayey soils which retain moisture and admit little air tend to warm up slowly. Organic matter, added to either heavy or light soils, will improve aggregation; clay soils, in particular, will then respond more quickly to temperature changes.

CLAY PARTICLES suspended in water ordinarily will sink to dense mass; with gypsum added particles will group together, leaving much larger pore spaces between particle clusters.

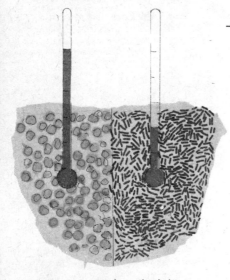

IN SPRING, sandy soils (left) warm up earlier than do clay soils (right).

AIR AND WATER IN THE SOIL

Water in the soil carries dissolved nutrients which are taken up by the roots; soil air provides a constant supply of oxygen to roots and to soil organisms in exchange for the carbon dioxide which they give off. In waterlogged soil there is little aeration, and plants suffer from lack of oxygen and a toxic carbon dioxide build-up.

An ideal soil for plant growth generally contains 50 per cent solid matter and 50 per cent pore space (the passageways between particles); moisture should occupy about one-half of the pore spaces and soil air the other half. Of the solid matter, roughly 45 per cent ideally should be mineral matter and 5 per cent organic.

Few garden soils meet these qualifications: Many are either too sandy or too clayey, giving a less-than-ideal balance between air and water in the pore spaces (as the amount of water in a soil goes up, the air supply goes down, and vice versa). Coarse-structured sandy soil has large spaces between particles; water drains through rapidly, leaving only that which clings as a film to individual particles. Clay soils, with much smaller particles, have a much greater total surface to which water can cling but will contain much less air because particles are packed closely together. Nearly all soils contain too little organic matter, and the amount is being reduced continually by decomposition.

HOW ORGANIC MATERIAL ENRICHES SOIL

We have emphasized only the mechanical improvement brought about by the addition of organic matter. Actually, the addition of once-living materials and the resultant improvement in structure also sets in motion a lively process—the decomposition of organic material by the action of soil microorganisms. In this decomposition, certain organic materials yield valuable nutrients which are essential for plant growth.

Organic matter, thus, has a dual relationship with the soil. When initially added, the effect of organic matter is purely physical; that is, soil structure is improved. Breakdown of the material then continues, with the rate of decomposition and the products of decay dependent upon the chemical composition of the organic matter itself.

Microorganisms within the earth are the soil's bacterial wrecking crews. They are constantly at work breaking down the complex compounds of decaying organic material into forms which can be taken up by growing plants as nutrients.

The organic matter in the soil acts as fuel for the soil bacteria. The bacterial fires they feed will smolder or flame, depending upon condition of the soil. The warmth, air, and water necessary to the activity of these bacteria (plants have these same requirements) are promoted by good soil structure. As soil temperatures increase in the spring, bacterial activity and population increase; and through their action, nutrients in the soil are made available to the plants.

When the organic matter is freshly added to the ground, a series of decay actions begins, and at each stage of breakdown different bacterial organisms work on the substance. This bacterial action is most intense on fresh material, and as decay action progresses the organic material finally reaches the fairly

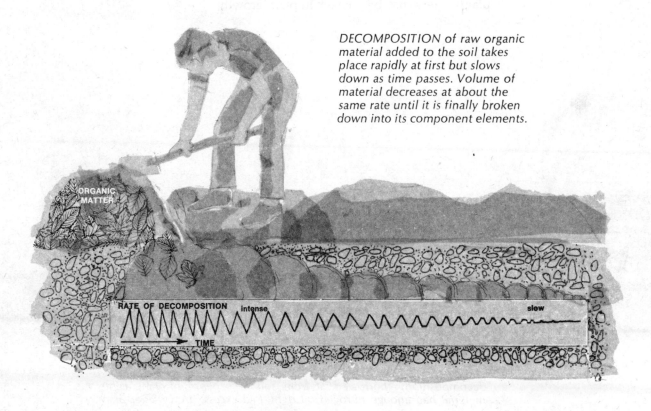

DECOMPOSITION of raw organic material added to the soil takes place rapidly at first but slows down as time passes. Volume of material decreases at about the same rate until it is finally broken down into its component elements.

stable, partially decomposed humus state. At this point, the rate of decomposition slows considerably, but humus itself eventually breaks down into its component elements and is lost as a structural conditioner. To maintain an organic level high enough to keep up good soil structure, new organic material must be added repeatedly.

The carbon/nitrogen ratio. The once-living organic matter in the soil is composed of a number of elements including carbon and nitrogen. The microorganisms in the soil feed upon this organic matter as they decompose it—using the carbon as energy fuel and nitrogen as building material for their bodies.

The relative amounts of these two elements are often compared, and the term carbon/nitrogen ratio is used to describe the relationship. To understand this term, suppose that a certain organic material is composed of 30 per cent carbon and 2 per cent nitrogen. The ratio of carbon to nitrogen is then 15 to 1 (obtained by dividing the percentages), or simply 15. Under natural conditions, microorganisms in the soil maintain a C/N ratio of about 10—that is, a rough balance of 10 parts of carbon to one part of available nitrogen.

This balance is upset when an organic material which is high in carbon and low in nitrogen, such as straw, is added to the soil. Because of the high carbon content, extra energy material is provided; the microorganism population is stimulated and increases in numbers. As these organisms use up the carbon for energy, they also need nitrogen to take care of their growing needs. If the amount of nitrogen in the organic material is insufficient to take care of these needs, the microorganisms must borrow nitrogen from the soil supply. This puts them in direct competition with plants which also need the nitrogen for growth. Therefore, if the supply of nitrogen in the soil is not sufficient to take care of the needs of both microorganisms and growing plants, there may be a check in plant growth.

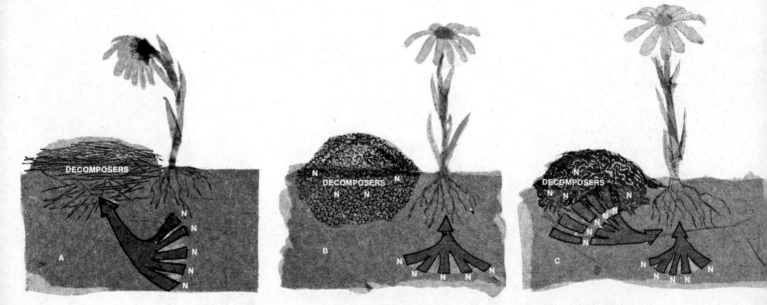

ORGANIC MATTER ADDED TO SOIL: at left, not enough nitrogen for decomposition, "borrowed" it from soil at expense of plant; center, material had enough nitrogen; at right, had excess, grew larger plant.

The loan of nitrogen to soil organisms is only temporary, but the nitrogen supply may be locked up in the bodies of the microorganisms when the plants need it most. During this period the carbon/nitrogen ratio is gradually being lowered as the organisms continue to use the carbon for energy. When the amount of carbon becomes insufficient to support the numbers of micro-organisms, they begin to die—their bodies decay and return the nitrogen to the soil.

Any organic material that contains at least 1.5 per cent nitrogen can take care of its own decomposition without reducing the total nitrogen supply in the soil. This includes organic materials with a carbon/nitrogen ratio at 30:1 or less.

IF NITROGEN is low in organic materials you add to your soil, you can add a natural nitrogen fertilizer (left) or spade material into soil during autumn months for spring planting.

In general, the legume (bean-pea family) plants are the highest in nitrogen content and have a low carbon/nitrogen ratio. Leaves and leaf mold, peat moss, garden compost, and manure (see pages 12-13) almost always contain sufficient quantities of nitrogen to provide for their own decay. In contrast, straw, sawdust (particularly redwood, fir, and pine), and grain stubble have high carbon/nitrogen ratios. In order to prevent a temporary depletion of nitrogen in your soil when using this latter type of organic material, the following procedures are recommended:

(1) Add a natural nitrogen fertilizer (see page 15) when using a carbon-rich, nitrogen-poor organic material. This is particularly important when fresh organic matter is added during the growing season. With extra nitrogen available, the bacterial activity will not temporarily deplete the nitrogen supply of the soil, and plant growth will not be retarded.

(2) If fresh organic matter is added to the soil, it is best to add it well ahead of planting to allow sufficient time for the nitrogen to be returned from the bacterial bodies to the soil. For this reason, many gardeners apply organic material in autumn. Decomposition begins then, and the nitrogen becomes anchored in the microorganisms during the winter; even though this is the time when some of the heaviest rains may occur, the nitrogen will not be leached away. In the spring, it will be slowly released into the soil during the time when the plants need it.

(3) When organic material is placed in a compost pile, the initial processes of decomposition occur outside the soil. By setting aside this special workshop for the bacteria, their supply of air, water, heat, and nitrogen can be more easily controlled, and organic matter partially broken down without disturbing the carbon/nitrogen balance in the garden soil.

COMPOSTING is best way to break down materials having high carbon/nitrogen ratios which would draw upon soil nitrogen to decompose.

EVALUATING ORGANIC SOIL ADDITIVES

The chart below lists the most generally available organic soil amendments. Not all, however, are equally valuable in all garden soils.

Sandy soils benefit most from addition of spongy materials that hold water and nutrients. Because water moves fast through sand, aeration is no problem. Wood products and the hulls of various crops offer the least help because they absorb less water than the other organic additives. The various peat mosses, on the other hand, absorb and retain water well and they decompose slowly, too. Intermediate in value are composts and the various manures; they supply some nutrients (which the peats do not) but they break down faster.

Clay soils present exactly the reverse demands and opportunities. With them, wood products serve well because they can physically separate clay particles without holding moisture like a sponge. Hulls from various crops do the same thing if finely ground or crushed. Any decomposing materials, however, ultimately break down to *humus* which, because of its sticky

CONDITIONERS SHOWN ACTUAL SIZE	CHARACTERISTICS	BEST USES	MUST YOU ADD NITROGEN?	HOW MUCH IS ASH?	NUTRIENT HOLDING
REDWOOD PRODUCTS	Granular, or granular-fibrous if bark used in mix. Flows, works in well. Low salinity, ash; high aeration. Long lasting, low cost	Best as soil conditioner or in container mix. Less good as mulch	To untreated redwood add ⅓ lb. **actual** nitrogen or 2½ lbs. organic fertilizer per 10 cubic feet	0.6 per cent	Fair
BARK	Granular. Easy to use. Low salinity, ash; high aeration. Long lasting. Higher cost than redwood. Douglas fir bark has splinters	Soil conditioner, excellent mulch; often used for orchids	To untreated bark add 1 lb. **actual** nitrogen or 8 lbs. organic fertilizer per 10 cubic feet	3 per cent	Fair
FIR SAWDUST	Granular. Easy to use. Low salinity, ash; high aeration. Long lasting, low cost. In bulk, untreated, may contain chips, shavings	Best as soil conditioner or in container mix. Less good as mulch	To untreated fir sawdust add ½ lb. **actual** nitrogen or 4 lbs. organic fertilizer per 10 cubic feet	2 per cent	Fair
LIGNIFIED WOOD	Granular. Easy to use. Moderate salinity, low ash; high aeration. Long lasting. High cost per unit volume, but less material needed	Best as soil conditioner or in container mix. Less good as mulch	None needed	2 per cent	Good
SPHAGNUM PEAT MOSS	Fibrous. Some treated for easy use. Some sold compressed. Low ash; good aeration. Highest water retention of conditioners listed	Best in container mix; good soil conditioner; less good as mulch	No need to add nitrogen	3 per cent	Very good

nature, will help bind together clay particles into larger aggregates—thereby improving drainage and aeration.

Is additional nitrogen needed? Many packaged wood products and sometimes those available in bulk are treated with nitrogen but in an inorganic form. Therefore, you will need to buy untreated wood products, and since untreated wood uses nitrogen as it decomposes you will have to add it. The chart tells how much organic nitrogen (in the form of blood meal) to add.

How much is ash? Organic material always contains a certain amount of mineral matter (ash) which is of questionable value in conditioning soil. The higher the percentage, the less efficient is the material. In some cases this mineral matter may be detrimental: Rice hulls, for example, contain a large amount of silicates which repel water.

Nutrient-holding capacity. The ability to hold nutrients is important in container soil mixes and in sandy garden soils where watering quickly leaches out nutrients. Wood products are not efficient nutrient holders. Peat mosses are best at holding nutrients and do not take nitrogen from the soil.

CONDITIONERS SHOWN ACTUAL SIZE	CHARACTERISTICS	BEST USES	MUST YOU ADD NITROGEN?	HOW MUCH IS ASH?	NUTRIENT HOLDING
HYPNUM PEAT MOSS	Fibrous. Less easy to work, more variable than sphagnum; higher nitrogen content. High ash. Lower cost than sphagnum	Container mixes; soil conditioner	Hypnum moss in its natural state contains some nitrogen	29.8 per cent	Excellent
SEDGE PEAT	Fibrous, variable. May be saline. High ash content. Sometimes subject to disease contamination. Low cost close to source	Soil conditioner where salts are not a problem	None needed	Varies: 30 to 50 per cent	Good
RICE HULLS	Easy-flowing, moderate ash, high potash. Very low cost where available, but considerable loss of volume when hollow hulls decompose	Potting mix, soil conditioner where available	To rice hulls add ⅛ lb. **actual** nitrogen or 2 lbs. organic fertilizer per 10 cubic feet	30 per cent	Poor
OAK LEAF MOLD	Variable and short-lived. May contain much undecomposed matter. In containers it adds to soil fertility, cuts feeding	Potting mix. Good for seeds when sifted. See page 31 for a precaution	None needed; actually contains some usable nutrients	30 per cent	Good
MANURE	High salinity, high ash. Use no more than 1 yard per 1,000 square feet. Low cost. Use with another conditioner as low grade fertilizer	Soil conditioner in sandy soils; useful mulch but odor may offend	None needed; manure is low grade fertilizer	Varies: about 50 per cent	Good

Plant Nutrition...
Using Organic Fertilizers

To improve your plants' growth, you may wish to give them nutrients by adding fertilizer to the soil. But whether the plants ever receive much of the nutrients contained in the fertilizer depends on the condition of the soil itself. A soil's physical characteristics and their relationship to organic materials are discussed in the previous chapter. Here, you can read about the essential ingredients of life called nutrients.

The essential nutrients for plant growth total sixteen and come from three primary sources: air, water, and soil. Plants get oxygen (O) and carbon (C) from the air, hydrogen (H) and oxygen from water. Except for nitrogen (N), soil supplies the remaining 13 nutrients; these are released as the soil's mineral particles gradually break down.

Organic matter also provides nutrients which are released through the action of decay organisms on the organic materials. Thus, soil structure and soil fertility go hand-in-hand—for as the organic materials added for structural improvement contribute nutrients, the soil's ability to act as a storage shed for nutrients increases as the structure improves.

Plants will grow well if enough of all 16 vital nutrients are available to the roots. But if one of the nutrients is deficient, the overall balance is upset and the plant will exhibit signs of the deficiency. Because plants need them in significantly greater quantities, three of the sixteen nutrients are considered major. These are nitrogen (N), phosphorus (P), and potassium (K).

NITROGEN—PLANTS NEED LOTS OF IT

The supply of nitrogen in the soil regulates a plant's ability to make *proteins* which are the growth promoters contained in each plant cell. This vital element promotes rapid growth of stems and leaves and gives plants a deep green color. An adequate nitrogen supply is especially important for growing good leaf crops, such as lettuce or cabbage. Unfortunately, nitrogen quickly gets leached or washed through soil beyond the range of plant roots; consequently, plants require nitrogen often and in relatively large quantities.

When there is not enough nitrogen to sustain new plant growth, this nutrient will move from the older plant cells to the newer, growing ones.

Older leaves will then turn yellow and may fall off. This yellowing and dropping of leaves farthest from the growing shoots is the primary symptom of nitrogen deficiency. A nitrogen deficiency also can produce stunted growth, smaller leaves, fewer flowers (and smaller fruit), and a delay in bud opening and development of flowers and leaves.

Because nitrogen is so vital to good plant growth, gardeners sometimes add too much nitrogen fertilizer to the soil. An oversupply of nitrogen makes plants grow too fast, become weak and spindly. With too much nitrogen, plants flower and fruit too late in their season. The resulting overleafy, thin-stemmed plants also may be more susceptible to disease, drought, and cold.

Nitrogen Cycle. The air we breathe is 80 per cent nitrogen (a gas). In fact, there may be more than 34,500 tons of this gas hanging over every acre of land. This inexhaustible supply remains fairly constant with nitrogen being returned to the atmosphere at approximately the same rate as it is removed.

Even with the gas in the atmosphere, your plants may be nitrogen starved because overhead nitrogen does nothing for plants. It must first combine with other elements.

In the soil, nitrogen is unique because it does not occur in mineral form. Instead, special soil bacteria can combine gaseous nitrogen from the air with other elements in a process called nitrogen fixation. Some of these nitrogen-fixing bacteria live in nodules on plant roots—chiefly on roots of *legumes*, such as peas. Others live freely within the soil.

While these bacteria "fix" nitrogen, other decay organisms release nitrogen as they break down organic matter. Nitrogen that enters the soil from dead plant and animal material undergoes several changes before plant roots can use it. First, microorganisms digest the raw organic nitrogen and convert it to a new form: *ammonia*. Other soil organisms then change ammonia to the *nitrite* form of nitrogen. And finally, still other microorganisms convert nitrite to the usable *nitrate* form.

Nitrogen Fertilizers

Below are listed some of the most commonly used organic nitrogen fertilizers. Remember that the coarser the grind, the longer it will be effective in your soil. Regardless of which one you use, results will be affected to a great extent by your soil and the weather. If your soil is cold, very wet, or too acid, the release may be extremely slow since the microorganisms that work on the conversion to nitrates do not prosper under these conditions. On the other hand, when soil is warm and moist the nitrogen release may be quite rapid. This fact minimizes the danger of succulent growth being produced at times of year when it could be damaged.

Blood meal. High nitrogen content (7 to 15 per cent). Can also be used as a liquid, mixed one tablespoon to a gallon of water.

Hoof and horn meal. High nitrogen content (7 to 15 per cent). Fine grinds popular for use in potting mixtures.

Cottonseed meal. Nitrogen content 6 to 9 per cent. Good for acid-loving plants in areas where soils are not already strongly acid.

Fish meal, fish emulsion. May contain up to 10 per cent nitrogen and nearly as much phosphorus. Some fish fertilizers have unpleasant odor.

How to Figure Actual Nitrogen

Fertilizing recommendations often call for a certain amount of actual nitrogen (as in, "apply 1 pound actual nitrogen per 1,000 square feet"). Here is how to calculate actual nitrogen or actual anything-else:
- *Look for the percentage of nitrogen (N) on the fertilizer label.*
- *Multiply that percentage times the weight of the fertilizer. For example, 10 pounds of blood meal (13 per cent nitrogen) contains 1.3 pounds actual nitrogen.*

Activated sewage sludge. Processed and sold by a number of cities; some is marketed nationally. Nitrogen content is 4 to 6 per cent, and the sludge also furnishes organic matter to soils.

Animal manures. Most kinds not as high in nitrogen as above-mentioned examples. Chief value is as an organic material to improve soil structure. All animal manures are safer to use, with reduced risk of burning plants, after they have decomposed or aged.

Bone meal. A phosphorus supplier, but may contain up to 5 per cent nitrogen.

AIR

Intake through the leaves:

- Oxygen ⎱ carbon dioxide
  Carbon ⎰ from air

SOIL

Intake through the roots:

- Hydrogen ⎱ from water
  Oxygen ⎰ and air

- Nitrogen ⎱ major nutrients
  Potassium ⎰ from minerals and
  Phosphorus ⎰ organic material

- Minor ⎱ usually present in soil
  elements ⎰

PHOSPHORUS—VITAL TO PLANT HEALTH

This nutrient is an active ingredient of the living material (protoplasm) in plant cells. Phosphorus is also necessary to the production of plant sugars (see page 18). In addition, it provides the mechanism by which energy, released by the burning of sugars, is transferred within the plant.

The weathering of soil particles as well as the decomposition of organic matter releases phosphorus into the soil. There, it exists in combination with other elements—particularly with oxygen as the phosphate ion.

The soil particles that contain phosphorus ions give them up reluctantly to the film of water (soil solution) that surrounds the particles. As the root tips grow into contact with the soil solution, they absorb the phosphorus that the solution is holding in available (that is, soluble) form.

A lack of available phosphorus in the soil has many of the same symptoms as nitrogen deficiency, but the leaves of a plant needing phosphorus are generally dull green with purple tints. Growth of the entire plant is dwarfed, root development is slow, maturity is delayed, and there is a lack (or poor quality) of fruit and seed development. In contrast to nitrogen, there is little danger of excess soil phosphorus.

The total phosphorus content of a soil can be a misleading figure, for when phosphate ions become available in the soil (either naturally or by application of organic matter or fertilizer) they can form some phosphate compounds which are so insoluble that plants can not use them. This is called phosphorus fixation, and it is more of a problem in definitely acid soils than in neutral or alkaline soils. If your soil is acid, you should raise its available phosphorus level to a point where the fixing power has been satisfied and there are no longer many "hungry" minerals, such as iron and aluminum, to combine with the phosphate ions.

Because of this fixation characteristic, there is little danger of loss of phosphorus through leaching.

Phosphorus Fertilizers

Bone meal. Most widely available supplier of phosphorus, averaging from 22 to 35 per cent phosphoric acid—with the added bonus of up to 5 per cent nitrogen. Steamed bone meal (the most common form sold) runs a little higher in phosphoric acid and lower in nitrogen.

Phosphate rock. A finely ground rock powder which contains roughly 30 per cent phosphoric acid plus many minor and trace nutrients.

POTASSIUM—ESSENTIAL TO LIFE PROCESSES

Often expressed as its compound *potash* (K_2O), potassium is essential to the life processes of plants, including the manufacture and movement of sugars and starches within the plant and to normal growth through the division of plant cells. Potassium is thought to hasten maturity and seed production and to aid in root development.

Except for nitrogen and calcium, plants remove from the soil more potassium than any other nutrient. Without sufficient potassium, plants tend to grow more slowly than is normal. While it is not always easy to detect the leaf pattern, plants that lack potassium often have leaves with mottled yellow tips and edges; older leaves look "scorched" at the edges.

Potassium in the soil exists in several forms. One form is soluble in water; other forms are insoluble and are unavailable to plants even though plants may grow in the soil for years.

Only about 1 per cent of the total supply of potassium in the soil can be drawn upon by plants. This important reservoir—called exchangeable potassium—may be derived from both minerals (soil particles) and organic matter. In this exchangeable form, potassium is not soluble and therefore is not free to move within the soil solution unless it undergoes a slow weathering process which releases ions into the solution. However, roots can pick up exchangeable potassium from the soil or humus particles without that element actually entering the soil solution.

Potassium Fertilizers

Granite dust, granite stone meal, potash rock. These supply up to about 8 per cent potash; amount varies somewhat according to the rock source. Also contain many minor and trace mineral nutrients.

Wood ashes. Hardwood ashes contain up to 10 per cent potash; softwood ash provides about half that much. Gather ashes as soon after burning as you can handle them. Store in a dry place, as potash is easily leached out. Don't use heavy applications, or a compacted, sticky soil structure can result.

OTHER VITAL NUTRIENTS

Calcium, magnesium, sulfur. These are secondary nutrients that are usually present in the soil in good supply. Calcium is necessary for manufacture and growth of plant cells, and aids in growth of root system. Magnesium is an important component of chlorophyll, the green material in the leaves of the living plant, which is necessary in order that photosynthesis might take place (see page 18). Sulfur, like nitrogen, is a protein provider.

Trace elements. Seven nutrients in the soil—iron, zinc, manganese, boron, molybdenum, copper, and chlorine—remain essentials for proper plant development but each is required only in small quantities. Usually there is no deficiency of these trace nutrients, except in situations of extreme soil acidity or alkalinity (see page 18). An ample supply of organic matter releases most of these elements to the soil.

THREE MAJOR NUTRIENTS at left (nitrogen, phosphorus, potassium) are together as necessary for plant nutrition as are all others, represented at right.

HOW PLANTS MANUFACTURE THEIR OWN FOOD

It is misleading to think of nutrients in the soil as plant "foods," even though this is a popular term for fertilizers. Actually, unlike animals, plants manufacture their own food through a process called photosynthesis. To make their food, plants take in energy from the sun, carbon dioxide from the air, and water from the soil; then they combine them to make plant sugars which can supply energy rapidly, or can be stored as food, or can be used as building material within the plant. Nutrients taken in from the soil help in the production of these plant sugars as well as in the building and growth of the plant.

While sugars are being manufactured, an opposite process also takes place. The sugar "fuel" supply is burned to provide enough energy to run all plant operations. In this burning-up process (respiration), oxygen is taken into the plant and carbon dioxide is released. Every part of the plant—from leaves to roots—must continually have enough energy to continue living.

Note that carbon dioxide—which is released in the burning up of sugars within the plant—also is taken in to build the plant sugars. The soil micro-organisms which break down organic materials operate in a similar manner to get energy: They use organic material for "fuel" and, as they break it down, take in oxygen and release carbon dioxide. In this way, the soil, the plant, and the atmosphere are very closely bound to one another.

PHOTOSYNTHESIS AND RESPIRATION are interdependent processes in which the products of each one are used in the processes of the other.

IS YOUR SOIL ACID OR ALKALINE?

In old-fashioned gardening terms, a soil is either sweet (alkaline) or sour (acid) —conditions which can be more accurately gauged by testing for *p*H. Chemically speaking, *p*H is a measurement of hydrogen ion concentration; gardeners need remember only that *p*H is a relative scale ranging from 1 to 14 with the midpoint of 7 as neutral. A soil is *acid* below 7 and *alkaline* (or basic) above 7. Soils in most low rainfall areas are alkaline; high rainfall areas tend toward acid soils.

Although some plants (such as rhododendrons and blueberries) prefer acid soils and others tolerate alkaline ones, most vegetables and flowers prefer soils that are neutral or slightly acid (*p*H 6.5). A slightly acid soil also is best for the availability of nutrients. At a lower *p*H (acid) availability of calcium, magnesium, and phosphorus decreases while manganese and aluminum may become too available and reach toxic concentrations. In alkaline soils at *p*H 8 or more, iron, copper, manganese, and zinc may become so unavailable that plant growth is impaired; phosphates may also be less available.

Soil Testing. Most gardens thrive without benefit of soil analysis. From observation, advice, and trial-and-error, the gardener usually discovers what will grow well in his soil and what care it needs to continue growing. For simple *p*H readings you can test the soil yourself with any of a number of manufactured kits.

If serious plant growth problems occur throughout your garden (or if you are about to plant a large area of questionable soil), you may want to arrange to have your soil analyzed. Professionally conducted, a soil analysis can point to the sources of trouble: poor irrigation practice, need for nutrients, presence of salinity or toxic substances in the soil, or attack by insects or disease. Your county agricultural agent's office probably can suggest a laboratory in your area that will test your soil and make recommendations for improvements.

Many interrelationships exist between organic (living) and inorganic (nonliving) parts of the plant world. The diagram below links together the interactions of organic matter, soil, nutrient availability, water, and air.

NUTRIENTS CYCLE

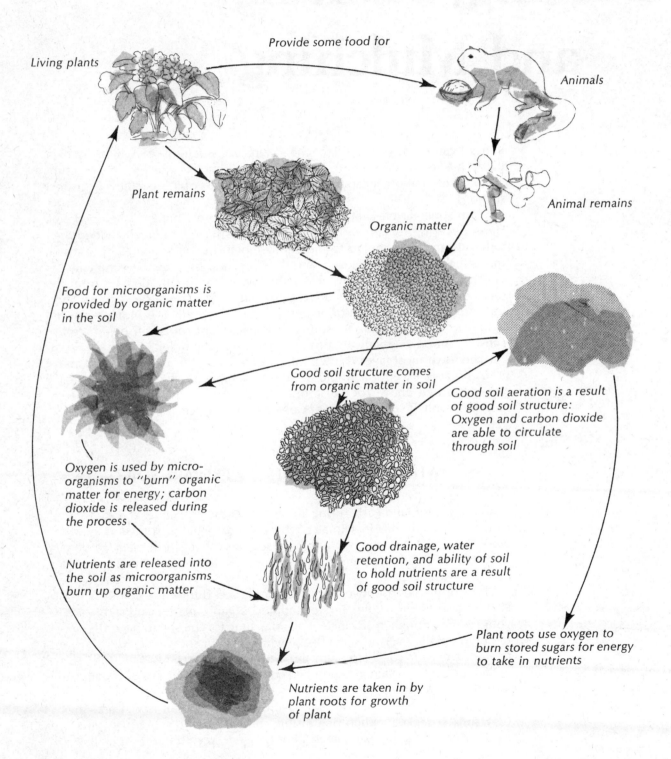

Provide some food for

Living plants

Animals

Plant remains

Animal remains

Organic matter

Food for microorganisms is provided by organic matter in the soil

Good soil structure comes from organic matter in soil

Good soil aeration is a result of good soil structure: Oxygen and carbon dioxide are able to circulate through soil

Oxygen is used by micro-organisms to "burn" organic matter for energy; carbon dioxide is released during the process

Good drainage, water retention, and ability of soil to hold nutrients are a result of good soil structure

Nutrients are released into the soil as microorganisms burn up organic matter

Plant roots use oxygen to burn stored sugars for energy to take in nutrients

Nutrients are taken in by plant roots for growth of plant

Digging, Planting, and Mulching

In most gardens if you could see the soil in cross-section, you would discover that it has its own distinctive "profile" something like a layer cake. In a simplified presentation, it can be considered to consist of three relatively distinct sections.

The upper layer—the topsoil—contains the most highly developed soil. Here, decaying remains of plants and animals have continually added their nutrients and contributed to the improvement of soil structure. As a result, this is the most fertile soil layer and is of the greatest value to your plants.

The region immediately below the topsoil is usually derived from the same basic material but has undergone much less change through weathering and the incorporation of organic remains. Typically it is more dense and lighter in color than the topsoil layer above. Plant roots can penetrate this subsoil, but only a relatively small proportion of them do.

The lowermost layer is often the parent material of the two layers above it. (A notable exception would be soils which have been moved by glaciers and deposited above rock of a different composition.) This layer is of importance only if somehow it appears near the surface.

WHEN ARE BEST TIMES TO PREPARE SOIL?

Autumn, winter, and early spring are generally the best times of year for you to prepare your soil. In climates where winter weather prevents outdoor work you will have only two optimum seasons for this, but many gardeners in the West, Southwest, and South will be able to take advantage of winter months as well.

Two principles are involved in preparing soil during the colder seasons. First, you are able to dig, aerate, and add organic matter and fertilizers to your soil far enough in advance of planting time for the soil to have an opportunity to "mellow". And second—the winter rain or snow will work with you to improve your soil's structure through weathering. Soil spaded in fall or winter and left in rough, unsmoothed condition should be crumbly and ready to plant come spring.

Whenever you work your soil, avoid days when soil is wet and sticky. Clay soils especially, when dug in this condition, tend to form compacted clods which resist breaking apart after they dry, resulting in a rock-like soil instead. A simple test before you dig is to pick up a handful of earth and squeeze it, then press this lump gently with a finger of your other hand. If the soil crumbles, it is ready to be worked; if the lump holds together, your soil is still too wet.

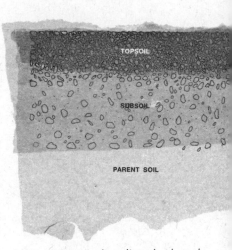

SOIL PROFILE of undisturbed earth shows darkest topsoil layer with organic matter, lighter subsoil layer with less organic materials, and lightest parent material layer below.

DIGGING ORGANIC MATERIAL INTO THE SOIL

To many gardeners, digging or turning the soil is simply rearranging that black dirt prior to planting something. For the person blessed with a deep topsoil this may be sufficient, as digging's primary function is to introduce air into the soil. However, a spade or fork takes about an 8 or 9-inch bite into the soil, and some topsoils—on previously uncultivated land—are not that deep; in such shallow soils, deep digging alone may actually decrease the value of the topsoil by mixing it with quantities of subsoil.

The majority of home gardeners will probably encounter a different soil situation: Most soils have been plowed, disced, harrowed, spaded, and forked for years so that there is no longer a sharp distinction between topsoil and subsoil. Another, and not uncommon, possibility is that the land may have been graded, leveled, or cut—leaving topsoil and subsoil thoroughly mixed, or with topsoil removed entirely.

No matter how thick your topsoil layer is, you should aim to keep at least one spade's depth in prime condition: crumbly, well-aerated, and amply fortified with organic matter. You'll know you have achieved this when you're able to insert a spade for its full depth into your soil with practically no effort.

Especially if you're preparing soil for annuals, vegetables, perennials, or a lawn it pays to think *big* in terms of organic matter quantity: If possible, add an amount of organic material equal to 25 to 50 per cent of the amount of soil you're preparing. This means that for the average spade's depth bite of 8 or 9 inches you ideally should incorporate from 4 to 8 inches of organic additives.

To do this, first dig your soil to the depth of your spade, shovel, or fork. Then, over the dug surface, spread the organic materials and dig them in. In order to get the benefit of a full spade's depth and still incorporate an organic layer 4-8 inches thick, spread about a 2-inch layer of organic additive and spade it in; repeat this process, in 2-inch layers, until you have incorporated all the organic materials necessary.

A spading fork (not a manure or hay fork) is the best tool for achieving even distribution of organic material through spaded soil. The soil and amendments filter through the tines and become blended as you dig.

If you use a spade or shovel to incorporate the organic additives, try not to invert the soil—leaving soil on top and organic material buried in a layer underneath. Instead, insert your spade and turn the soil to one side or the other; in turning, the organic additives will sift down the face of the soil and be distributed to the full spade's depth.

If your topsoil is shallow, lacking, or thoroughly mixed with subsoil it may take you several years to put your soil into prime condition. But even during the formative period you'll be rewarded with better and better plant growth. In each subsequent working of what was your organically impoverished soil, incorporate at least 25 per cent by volume of organic materials.

TO INCORPORATE ORGANIC matter into soil with spade, insert tool into soil at slight angle, turn spadeful of soil to right or left against unspaded soil; this distributes organic materials evenly throughout spaded depth.

DIGGING SOIL will incorporate organic materials, both dried weeds (shown here) and materials spread onto surface. Digging also aerates soil for better root growth.

EASY SOIL PREPARATION in two steps: first, spread organic materials on soil surface (left); then, blend them in with a rotary tiller (right).

Double Digging

Reduced to its basic principles, this is double digging (also called "trenching"): Remove a spade's depth of soil over all the area you want to improve and put it aside. Dig organic materials into the next spade's depth. Mix the same organic materials into the soil you initially removed and put that mixture on top of the deeper mixture. What you accomplish is aeration of your soil to a depth of approximately 18 inches with the inclusion of organic matter as well. Deep root penetration is easier, so that deep-rooted plants will reward you with better growth.

Admittedly this involves a lot of back-straining labor which, although always beneficial to the soil, may be unnecessary for many plants. Its special value is for deeply-rooted perennial plants which will grow in one place for several years, and for deeply-rooted shrubs which will be permanent. Roses stand as a classic example of a popular plant which responds mightily to such careful preparation.

All you need for double digging is a spade or spading fork, perhaps a pick or a mattock for the tough second layer, and endurance. Details for the traditional method are shown in the drawing below.

TRADITIONAL DOUBLE-DIGGING method is to dig out a trench of soil to a spade's depth and lay it aside (1). Next, dig the soil in the bottom of the trench 2 to a spade's depth and incorporate organic materials. Then take the spade's-depth trench 3, place it on area 2 and dig in organic matter. Treat area 4 as you did area 2, area 5 as you did area 3. When you reach the end of your bed, soil put aside from trench 1 will fill the final trench.

PREPARING THE SOIL AT PLANTING TIME

How you prepare your soil for planting will be determined by what types of plants you intend to grow. The listings on pages 55-71 present simple instructions for planting and general maintenance of many vegetables, fruits and ornamentals; the following guidelines will help you plan your garden preparation.

Annuals and Vegetables

Because annuals and most vegetable crops complete their growth cycle within one growing season, the soil in which you plant them will need to be in the best possible condition and should contain most of the nutrients the plants will require. Unlike the growing of woody plants or even perennials,

CALICHE

If you are gardening in the arid Southwest, you may be familiar with—or may encounter—a soil condition called *caliche*. This is a layer of calcium carbonate (lime) found usually beneath the soil surface; the name is derived from the Latin word for lime. Caliche can vary in texture from granular to solid and cementlike; its thickness will range from only several inches (if you're lucky) to many feet.

Typically, caliche forms an impervious layer beneath a surface layer of soil which you can cultivate and a region of porous subsoil. The troubles it creates are: Roots cannot penetrate caliche, and water will not drain through it. If the caliche in your garden is only a few inches thick you can dig down to it, break it up with a pick, and discard it; then, you can garden normally. However, to plant trees, shrubs, or hedges where caliche is hard and thick, you either have to bore through it and discard the borings (to provide for drainage and root penetration) or plant above it in raised beds. The drawings below show how to dig holes with a power auger and plant a container-grown shrub or tree. You also can make large holes with a backhoe.

First, bore through the caliche to a porous substratum, if this is possible. It is essential that you penetrate *through* the caliche; otherwise you will create nothing more than an oversized, subterranean container with no drainage. Having done this, remove and discard the caliche.

For large trees, make the planting hole 4 to 6 feet wide and 3 to 5 feet deep; smaller trees or shrubs will need holes about 4 feet wide and 3 feet deep. In preparing flower beds, dig 2 feet deep and put drainage holes every 6 to 8 feet (for rose beds, every 4 to 6 feet).

For hedge planting it is easiest to use a trencher, making a trench 2 feet wide and deep with drainage holes spaced every 12 to 15 feet.

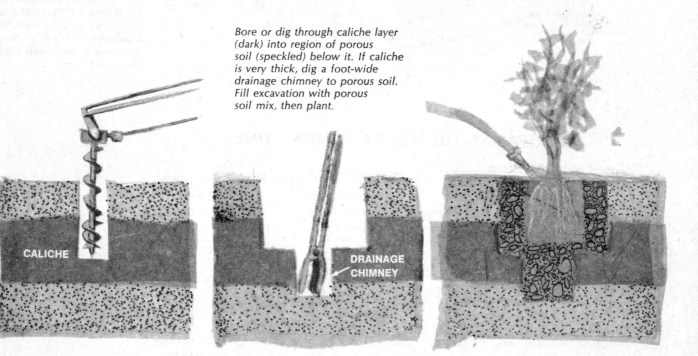

Bore or dig through caliche layer (dark) into region of porous soil (speckled) below it. If caliche is very thick, dig a foot-wide drainage chimney to porous soil. Fill excavation with porous soil mix, then plant.

CALICHE

DRAINAGE CHIMNEY

you will not have the opportunity to improve the soil gradually after the plants are in.

For most of these single-season plants, the directions given for soil preparation under "Digging" on page 21 are sufficient. Any individual instructions differing from the basic recommendations will be covered in the listings beginning on page 55.

Since these plants will last but one season, your organic soil additives need not be the longest lasting materials you can obtain. A material which is relatively quick to break down—sawdust, for example—may be more directly beneficial to these plants: The greater amount of nutrients released during the more-rapid decomposition can be quickly and easily used by the plants.

Most annuals and many vegetables will need a ready supply of nitrogen and phosphorus; these are the two nutrients most closely associated with growth and the production of flowers and fruit. Root crops, such as potatoes or onions, will require proportionately less nitrogen and more potassium. For specific fertilizer directions see the listings on pages 55-71.

WELL-PREPARED, crumbly soil with plenty of organic matter is one key to success with single-season plants.

Perennials, Bulbs, and Bulb-Like Plants

In contrast to the single-season annuals and vegetables, perennial plants will remain in place, undisturbed, for several to many years. What you need to provide for them, then, is a well-structured soil that will remain so for the life of your perennial planting.

If you have the time and the energy, try double digging your future perennial bed (see page 23). Many perennial roots go deeper than the usual

FOR TRUE BULBS, plant single bulb about 3 times as deep as its greatest diameter; mix in a generous tablespoon of bonemeal in bottom of hole.

EASY BULB PLANTING for large number of bulbs is to excavate prepared soil to proper planting depth, then position bulbs and cover.

spade's-depth preparation of garden soil. The increase in aeration, improvement in drainage, and supply of organic nutrients at this depth will promote more and deeper rooting—hence stronger, tougher plants.

Organic additives that decompose slowly maintain good soil structure over a long period. Bark products in heavier soils and some peats in sandier ones will serve this purpose well. The bark products help *separate* closely packed clay particles, thereby aiding drainage and aeration; peats fill in the spaces between sand particles while also holding moisture and nutrients in this otherwise fast-draining soil.

Incorporation of various fertilizers at soil preparation time should be no less thorough than for an annual bed (see page 23), but you will not always be able to provide enough to last through the life of a perennial planting. Phosphorus and potassium—derived from rock powders—may last for a number of years, but it is important that you replenish nitrogen periodically (see page 15).

Many perennial plantings will benefit greatly from an organic mulch (see page 31). Mulching will help to maintain a soil environment favorable to plant growth, providing fairly consistent moisture when sun and wind would dry the soil and protection from beating by heavy rain or sprinkler drops.

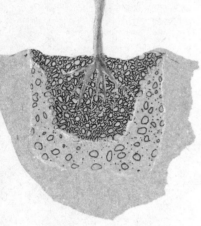

IN HEAVY SOIL for bare root planting if you add organic matter to root-zone soil you will need transitional soil between root zone and heavy native soil.

Shrubs and Trees

If you could muster the time, energy, and organic materials, the ideal way to prepare soil for shrub and tree plantings would be by double digging the entire area their roots ultimately would occupy (see page 23). Very often however, this is impractical. Soil improvement for tree and shrub planting is usually limited to a soil zone about twice to three times the size of the plant's root ball at that moment.

You will plant your trees and shrubs in one of two ways: bare-root; or with the roots in soil (either from a container or balled-and-burlapped, dug from a growing field). Each method has a few special pointers.

Bare-root planting is the usual method for a number of familiar garden plants: roses, deciduous flowering shrubs, deciduous fruit and shade trees, and cane fruits. These are ready to plant during their dormant seasons—late fall through winter to early spring in mild climates, fall or spring where winters are more severe.

When you plant a bare-root specimen you usually can and should refill the entire hole with one uniform soil. By contrast, when you plant a container plant you actually put two different soils in the planting hole—the soil that is in the container root ball, and the other soil with which you refill the soil around the root ball (see next page).

If your soil is heavy and you mix a lot of organic matter with it and then place the mixture around the plant's bare roots, the planting hole can become a "container" for the new plant. Roots will be unable to grow easily into the more dense surrounding soil, and water applied to the new plant will not drain into neighboring soil as fast as the prepared soil takes it in. The result—waterlogged root zone, dead roots.

Even the most dedicated organic gardener need not add anything to the soil going back into the hole around bare roots unless some unusual circum-

BARE ROOT PLANTING where native soil is light: add organic matter to root-zone soil.

stance warrants it. Remember that almost all deciduous fruit orchards and almost all rose gardens—"organic" or otherwise—were planted with the local soil, and nothing added, going back into the hole around the roots.

The unusual circumstances, and what to do about them: If your soil is sandy to a medium loam (hence well-drained), you can safely fill the planting hole with a mixture of half organic matter and half native soil. For heavier, less well-drained soils you'll need to use the generously-amended soil only in the immediate root zone, while filling in the bottom and sides of the hole with a "transition zone" soil composed of the native soil with no more than 25 per cent organic matter mixed in.

Since planting time is your only opportunity to add organic phosphorus and potash to the plant's root zone, it is especially important that you incorporate these two nutrients into the soil when planting shrubs and trees that presumably will not be moved.

Planting balled-and-burlapped plants or plants from containers seldom presents the ideal situation in which the soil in the root ball exactly matches the garden soil in structure. Nursery plants are grown in a wide variety of specially-mixed soils. Much of container-grown stock is planted in a light mixture composed of sand and organic matter (usually ground bark or peat moss) or similar mixtures with some loam added. Field-grown stock, on the other hand, is usually grown in a much heavier soil, so that it is easier to dig, wrap roots in burlap, and handle without danger of breaking the ball.

In either case, if the soil in the root ball differs much from the garden soil in which you're planting, your goal will be the same. To make a gradual transition from light to heavy (or vice versa), mix a soil of intermediate structure for use in back-filling around the root ball. If the soil within the root ball is light and the garden soil is heavy, add organic matter (up to half the total volume in the case of very heavy garden soil). When the root ball soil is heavy and the garden soil very light, it's advisable to add some loam and organic matter to the transition zone soil.

The same fertilizer recommendations for bare-root planting (see above) apply here, too.

BARE ROOT PLANTING calls for large hole to spread roots out, organic materials, and a stick (or shovel handle) to position plant to nursery depth.

CONTAINER-GROWN and balled-and-burlapped plants usually need a transition zone soil between root ball and garden soil.

HANDLE container-grown plant (left) with care to keep root ball intact; leave burlap on balled-and-burlapped plants when planting them.

Preparing Soil for Lawn Planting

Soil for a healthy lawn should be of uniform structure to a depth of 8-12 inches. If you add topsoil to correct grade or contour, it should be *thoroughly* mixed with the existing soil to avoid creating an "interface" (a plane where two soils meet) which could interfere with good drainage and root growth.

Before you begin to prepare your lawn seedbed you should have your soil tested to determine its acidity or alkalinity. If the *p*H is below 5.5, add lime (calcium carbonate is best) at the rate of 50-75 pounds for every 1,000 square feet; apply it with a spreader to dry soil. If *p*H is above 8.0 (strongly alkaline), add soil sulfur at 10 pounds to each 1,000 square feet, incorporating the material into the top six inches of soil. Consult your county agricultural agent or a commercial soil laboratory if your soil's *p*H is above 8.5.

To achieve uniform structure in the top 12 inches of soil—for optimum water penetration, nutrient-holding ability, and root penetration—add 30 to 50 per cent by volume of organic materials to the soil. Three inches of amendment mixed with the top six inches of soil makes a 33 per cent mixture. If you use raw sawdust or bark, you will have to supply additional nitrogen to aid the initial decomposition (see "carbon/nitrogen ratio" on page 10); use 12 pounds of actual nitrogen (see page 15) for every 1,000 square feet where sawdust or bark is laid three inches deep. If you add nitrogen in the form of manure to raw materials to hasten decomposition, you should keep the seedbed moist for at least 30 days prior to seeding. Failure to do so may produce a temporary salinity which could be harmful to germination and subsequent growth.

Although you can't possibly add enough nitrogen to last the life of your lawn, you should add enough to sustain the grass right after it sprouts. This can be added along with organic materials, or it can be spread on the finished seedbed. See page 71 for specific directions.

Following the preparation of the soil with organic matter and fertilizer, the next step is to level and smooth the surface. Rake the soil first, removing all stones and other foreign material and either removing or breaking up any clods. Then, drag the soil with any one of the illustrated devices to eliminate high spots and fill in low ones. After raking and dragging, go over the smoothed surface in two directions with a full roller. If rolling turns up low spots, rake or drag the soil and roll it again. Soil is now ready for seeding (see page 71).

ROLLING is a necessary operation both when planting a sod lawn and when preparing a lawn seedbed.

THREE LEVELING DEVICES for preparing a lawn seedbed: rectangular frame (left), overlapping boards (center), straight-edge T (right).

HOW TO START SEEDS

There are several advantages to starting seeds in flats or other containers. It is the best method to use for expensive or very fine seed, for seed that takes a long time to germinate and grow (this includes most perennials), and–if you keep the flats indoors–for some annuals and vegetables that you want to start early when the outside temperature is too cold or the weather too wet. It also enables you to grow numerous varieties not normally found in the market or at nurseries, including some really flavorful old vegetables still sold by specialty seed firms but not available as produce because they either ship or store poorly.

You have to wait about 2½ to 4 months to get bloom from most annuals started from seed in April; this may include up to 8 to 10 weeks in the flat, from the time you sow seed until the plants are ready to set out in the garden. Therefore, get your seed started as soon as possible, timing your efforts so the young plants will be ready to set out when the weather will keep them actively growing. (Seedlings started *too* early, and set out when soil is still cold, will just sit there until the soil warms up to their liking.)

Seed-starting soil mixes should be loose, drain well (and shouldn't cake like clay), yet hold moisture. Equal parts of coarse sand, peat moss or fine ground bark or compost, and garden loam make a good basic mix; screen it through a ¼-inch mesh. Some gardeners prefer to eliminate compost and soil in order to avoid any problem with damping-off (a soil disease that attacks seed and tiny seedlings), or to plant in an entirely sterile medium such as vermiculite. You can sterilize a mix by baking it in an oven at 160°-180° for two hours, but the baking process gives off a terrible, permeating odor.

Make sure the flat or pot has holes or open spaces at the bottom for drainage. Then, fill to about ½ inch from the top with the mixture you have prepared. Firm with a block of wood and mark off rows about 2 inches apart with a piece of lath or a pencil, pressing ⅛ to ¼ inch deep into the mix. (If seed is fine, check the seed packet—most fine seeds should not be buried, and may be broadcast over the soil surface.) Cover seeds (to a depth roughly equal to twice their diameter) by sifting, through a fine sifter such as a window screen, a mixture of half sand and half peat moss or ground bark or compost. Press down the surface gently but firmly with a flat board, then water gently so as not to disturb the seeds. If you have a tub or sink, put 1 to 2 inches of water in it and place the seed flat in it to soak the needed water up from the bottom.

Cover the flat or pot with a sheet of newspaper and a pane of glass, or with a piece of wet burlap or newspaper; then place in a warm, protected spot but not in direct sunlight. Keep the seeding mixture moist but not soaking wet. Check for germination in about 4 or 5 days, and as soon as the first seedlings appear, remove the covering and give full light but not direct sun.

When the seedlings have two sets of true leaves you should move them to another flat or pot where they will have room to grow large enough to be planted in the garden. In this flat use a slightly richer soil mix, such as 2 parts loam, 1 part sand, and 1 part peat moss, compost, or ground bark. Punch holes in the mix deep enough to accommodate seedling roots without crowding and about 2 inches apart each way. Insert roots, firm soil around them (using a finger or small stick), then water gently. Shade the plants and keep them out of drafts for several days until they are over the shock of transplanting. When they have grown so that their leaves touch and shade the soil, they are ready to plant in the garden.

Seed-planting soil mix is firmed into flat (top) prior to seeding; areas are marked off (center) for different seeds, and seeds are sown; finally, seeds are covered with screened soil mixture (bottom), then carefully watered.

MULCHING

What's a mulch? It's any material that you place on the soil surface to conserve moisture, to keep soil temperatures relatively constant around plant roots, to prevent erosion, to keep fruits, flowers, or leaves clean, or to reduce weed growth. Mulching to control weeds is safer than cultivation, which may damage tender surface roots. It can be either an organic substance such as ground bark, sawdust, or shavings, or it can be an inorganic material such as crushed rock or beach pebbles.

Organic mulches decompose and thereby furnish some humus that improves the soil's structure. In addition, decomposing organic mulches contribute to the soil's nutrient supply by adding small amounts of nitrogen, phosphorus, potassium, and minor elements.

You can spade old mulches into flower and vegetable beds each year to increase the humus content of the soil. Then, when the weather warms, spread a new mulch. Some gardeners follow a year-round mulch program, continually adding new materials to the surface as the mulch in contact with the soil decomposes. By doing this, many have eliminated—after several years—the need for digging the soil before planting vegetables and flowers. The constantly decomposing mulch keeps the topsoil in prime condition for root growth.

Mulch management involves relatively little trouble. Depending on the material, spread mulches from 2 to 6 inches deep. Usually, the denser or finer the material, the less you need. Two inches of sawdust might have the same effect as, say, 6 inches of straw. Mulches should be deeper around trees and shrubs than in flower or vegetable beds. Add to organic mulches each year to keep them at the desired depth.

Although mulches retain moisture, you still need to water plants growing in the mulched soils. Check regularly for moisture with your fingers or a soil sampling tube, and water thoroughly when needed.

PLASTIC MULCH around young vegetable plants will help get them off to a good start by keeping root zone moist and soil temperature even.

ORGANIC MULCH is especially beneficial to young plants whose foliage has not grown enough to shade bare soil around them.

For several specific situations a word of caution is in order. If mulching makes soil too moist for certain plants, don't mulch them. Newly-planted seedlings and some perennials can damp off or rot at the crown, respectively, if the soil remains too moist—especially when the temperature is high. Wait until seedlings have been planted for several weeks before mulching. For rot-prone perennials (such as delphinium and aconite), keep a mulch away from the bases of plants, although surrounding soil may be covered.

Organic Mulches

Many materials make useful mulches. Some of them are plentiful enough to be available to gardeners everywhere. Others are by-products in local areas, are often seasonal in supply, and therefore are not widely distributed.

Partially decomposed compost. If you have a compost pile you will find that some of the less decomposed material is about the right texture to use as a mulch. Save the fine-screened, crumbly compost for soil conditioning, seed planting, container mixes, and small critical mulching jobs.

Grass clippings can be used before seed has ripened—otherwise they may introduce weeds and lawn grass to planting areas. Spread the clippings in a thin layer which will allow them to dry; if applied too thickly they will quickly mat down, become slimy, build up heat, and develop objectionable odors in the decomposition process. Flies can and do breed in thickly-piled grass clippings.

Ground bark, mostly from fir, pine, and hemlock trees, is usually reddish brown in color and makes an attractive, long-lasting cover. It is sold in sizes that range from 2-inch chunks to a very fine grind.

Leaf mold is an excellent but expensive mulch useful where you would like to maintain or increase the acidity of your soil. In California, the oak root fungus (Armillaria) can be a particular threat to many garden plants; there, you should use oak leaf mold with caution as chunks of wood the size of your finger or larger among the leaves can introduce the fungus to your soil. It is also found in other areas but is much less of a problem.

Manure may add some nutrients, but if too fresh it may heat up and burn plants. Basically, the value of any manure, in terms of its nitrogen content, depends on what the animal has been eating, so nitrogen percentages will fluctuate. Packaged steer manure may contain weed seeds and also large amounts of salts that can damage plants (see page 33).

Peat moss is satisfactory if you apply and maintain it properly but can become a liability if you mishandle it. Although it absorbs and holds water, it is often dry and dusty when you get it, and you must knead it and squeeze it to get water into its spongy tissues. Do this before you apply it as a mulch. If a properly-applied peat moss mulch dries out it is difficult to re-moisten; water may run off the mulch surface instead of soaking into the soil beneath.

Pine needles begin green, then turn reddish brown to gray; they last long and make a good mulch around acid-loving plants such as azaleas, rhododendrons, and camellias. When thoroughly dry they can be a fire hazard.

MULCH AROUND VEGETABLES prevents soil from drying out rapidly, promotes steady growth which they require.

Redwood bark, with its fibrous texture, makes an attractive, durable mulch. It stays in place and has a good looking, dark red color when moist. It may repel water (like a duck's back) to some degree.

Redwood chips make a decorative, long-lasting mulch, their red to brown color slowly graying with age. The 1/8 to 1-inch-wide chips lie flat and do not easily blow away.

Redwood shavings last long and do not mat down as much as sawdust; however, they may blow away in a strong wind. Shavings from other trees usually break down more rapidly than those from redwoods.

Sawdust is easy to handle and covers the ground well. New sawdust is very high in carbon and low in nitrogen (see carbon/nitrogen ratio, page 10) and will draw upon the soil nitrogen as the lower surface decomposes. To compensate for this and insure enough nitrogen for plants in the area, apply 1/2 pound of actual nitrogen (see page 15) to 100 square feet for every inch of mulch depth. Manufacturers of packaged sawdust often add nitrogen to the sawdust before it is bagged and shipped to retail outlets; most if not all of this nitrogen fortification is with inorganic nitrogen.

Straw, hay, cured grasses. Straw is a good, long-lasting mulch that breaks down slowly but it has a high carbon/nitrogen ratio close to sawdust. To offset any nitrogen depletion from straw decomposition add the same amount of nitrogen as is recommended above for raw sawdust. Long grasses such as bluegrass, timothy, rye grass, or wild hay serve well as mulches; cut them before the seed ripens. Alfalfa will give you a mulch that contains a valuable amount of nitrogen.

In areas where they are readily available and inexpensive, the following organic materials are often used as mulches: cottonseed hulls, rice hulls, cocoa bean hulls (which have a chocolaty aroma), almond hulls, coffee grounds, mushroom compost, spent hops, tanbark, apple pomace, grape pomace, sugar cane bagasse, ground corncobs, and many more.

Inorganic Mulches

These materials add neither nutrients nor humus to the soil but are otherwise effective mulches. Several are permanent and attractive.

Gravel and sand make attractive mulches. They are usually spread 2 to 4 inches deep and are quite permanent once they are installed.

Plastic sheeting is sometimes used in vegetable beds or in areas where its appearance won't be objectionable. You can spread it in strips on both sides of a planting row or lay it in a sheet over the soil and punch holes through it for planting. Black plastic prevents soil temperature fluctuation, stops weed growth, and slows the drying out of soil.

Rock of many sizes, shapes, colors, and origins can make a permanent covering that is especially advantageous around trees that are subject to crown rot. Spread rocks deeply and you'll be able to walk on them almost immediately after watering without getting your shoes wet or dirty. One word of caution: Under pine and other fine-needled trees it is difficult to keep rock mulches clean.

NATURAL STONE MULCH under tree keeps root zone cool, allows easy water penetration to soil, and is both good-looking and permanent.

STEER MANURE—PROS AND CONS

In much of the United States, cattle are still pastured. But in the West, and particularly in California, pressures on land have forced dairy as well as feedlot cattle to be kept in corrals where feed is trucked to them. The manure from these dairies and feedlots is regularly picked up and hauled off to several locations where it literally forms mountains which are allowed to compost and age for over a year before being sold.

Although most, if not all, bagged manure is sold as "steer manure," much of it comes from dairy herds. Perhaps in years past the manure from stockyard animals may have had a slightly higher nitrogen content because of the high-protein feed used to fatten the cattle; but today many dairies also feed their animals a high protein diet, thereby erasing the one possible real distinction between the two manures.

Man's long history of using cattle manure in and on the soil has created the lasting belief that the material is both a fertilizer and a soil conditioner. To a certain extent it does both of these jobs—providing its limitations are clearly understood.

The foremost limitation to the use of manure derived from animals kept in restricted quarters is the high salt content. Tests run on over a dozen samples of bagged steer manure contained from 5.05 to 8.86 per cent soluble salts, based on dry weight. Salts in this quantity in contact with roots can stunt or kill plants.

Why salts are a significant problem in a material that has been used successfully for centuries has two probable answers (the difficulty in being completely positive is because there are no thorough analyses of cattle manure from, say, a hundred years ago). First, the manure-using farmlands of Europe and the eastern United States get considerably more rainfall than the southwestern states. There undoubtedly were salts in the old-country manure, but regular rainfall would have leached them out—in the barnyard and after it was spread. Second, cattlemen and dairymen today know definitely an animal's daily salt and mineral requirements and often put enough salt and other minerals in the daily feed ration to make sure the animal gets its needed allowance. In addition, they give the animals free access to block or granulated salt, their drinking water contains some soluble salts, and a little salt is present in their feed. Therefore, it is obvious how an animal today can take in more salt than is its daily salt requirement. The excess taken in can only go right on through the animal.

In areas of the Southwest where salts tend to build up in the soil, liberal use of manure compounds the problem. The natural solution is to leach the salts from the manure by generous waterings, but the leaching that is necessary to wash out salts will likely wash out much of the nitrogen. In the long run, manure that is made safe by having salts washed out probably supplies only some phosphate and potash plus a fair quantity of organic matter to improve soil structure.

Since manure's fertilizer value (in terms of nitrogen) will most likely be negligible—or at best merely an added bonus—its real uses will be confined to employment as a mulch and as a soil amendment. As mulch, or as a cover for seed of "winter grass" sown on Bermuda lawns in fall, use it at the rate of $1/2$ cubic yard ($13^1/2$ cubic feet) to 1,000 square feet of surface area. For a soil conditioner, never use quantities greater than 8 cubic feet per 100 cubic feet of cultivated soil with leaching ($1/2$-inch applied to the surface and mixed 6 inches deep), or no greater than $5^1/2$ cubic feet per 100 cubic feet of soil without leaching.

Mountain of manure (top), collected from dairies and feedlots, decomposes for a year or more, then may be bagged for sale as steer or dairy manure (bottom).

EARTHWORMS—LIVING SOIL CONDITIONERS

Earthworms have several valuable uses for the organic gardener. They adapt, when properly cared for, to large gardens, to patio beds, or even to the confines of containers—as long as no toxic materials permeate the soil. Their tunnels provide a ventilating system which allows oxygen and water to penetrate the soil more easily, and makes it easier for roots to grow deeper. This more-absorbent soil also helps prevent excessive erosion due to water run-off.

All earthworms, as they burrow and feed, swallow quantities of soil and organic matter, digest it, extract its food value, and expel the residue as a manure called worm casts. These casts are about five times richer in nitrates than the top 6 inches of average garden soil, are twice as rich in exchangeable calcium, seven times richer in available phosphorus, and eleven times richer in available potassium.

There are at least three kinds of earthworms found in North America—the large, fat "night crawler" that is so well-known in the Rocky Mountain area; a smaller red kind; and a blue-gray, rather thin worm. Usually you will find them in garden soils that are in good condition. None of these, it seems, can be bred in captivity to be sold for soil conditioning: They only thrive in the kind of soil in which they are born, neither migrating nor adapting from one soil type to another. In addition, they will not live in fresh manure or raw compost. The night crawler may be as much of a nuisance as it is a benefit because it deposits really large amounts of soil on the surface nightly.

The worm most often sold is known by several names—among them, Red Wiggler and Red Hybrid (although whether there is such a thing as a hybrid worm is doubtful). This is the worm most valuable in helping to break down raw materials in a compost pile. Given plenty of fresh manure and compost, they will remain and thrive in your garden. These worms are rather short, thick, and red; their main function is the breakdown of raw organic materials. To establish them in your compost pile, place a large bucketful of these worms from a commercial grower in the center of the pile—they can double in number about every 30 days. However, remember this caution: Make sure your compost pile is through heating, as the high temperatures will kill them immediately. When using red worms in composting you may find that no turning is necessary; at any rate, the aeration that their tunneling provides will aid the production of only the odorless, aerobic bacteria (see pages 36-43).

The red worms generally will not multiply in the soil unless generous amounts of fresh manure or compost are available to them in the form of a mulch. As long as manure or compost is applied to moist soil the worms will continue to reproduce and do their beneficial soil work. When weather is below freezing or extremely dry, the worms will burrow deeper and hibernate.

To establish red worms in tree or shrub plantings, dig 6-inch-diameter holes a foot deep and 2-3 feet apart at the drip lines of the plants' branches; fill with worms and compost. Heavily mulch the area with manure or compost and cover lightly with grass clippings or hay. In beds of annuals or perennials, plant the worms in holes spaced 4-5 feet along the beds and mulch with organic materials such as manure or compost. This organic mulch insures the spread of red worms through the entire bed, and makes a more suitable climate for the increase of your native garden worms.

WATERING—OFTEN MISUNDERSTOOD

You can not partially wet soil. A small amount of water will completely moisten a small amount of soil but never partially wet a large area. Many gardeners fail to understand this fact and water lightly. Water supplied to the surface must moisten the topmost layer to its capacity before passing through to the next. Therefore, with a light sprinkling of water, the lower levels of the soil aren't even reached. So, you should water deeply and then avoid watering again until the soil is somewhat dry. That way you give the soil a chance to take in a good supply of air as the water supply is slowly removed.

Each type of soil has its own water-holding capacity; the soil's texture (that is, whether it is composed of coarse, medium, or fine particles) determines the amount of water that should be applied. For example, consider a shrub, around which is a 2-foot diameter watering basin; fill this basin with water from a 3-gallon watering can. In a clay soil—because water drains slowly—it is tempting to think that one canful provides sufficient water. But actually, if the shrub had already removed most of the water from the soil to the full depth of its root growth, that one canful would moisten the soil only to a depth of 3 inches. If, instead of a shrub, you were watering a tomato nearing full growth with a root penetration to 6 feet, it would require 12 canfuls, or 36 gallons, for proper irrigation.

This does not mean that the water bill for a clay soil will be greater than that for a sandy soil. Fortunately, the greater the water-holding capacity of the soil, the less frequently it requires water. Consequently, a sandy soil must be filled more than twice as often as a clay soil. Increasing the water-holding capacity in lighter soils by adding organic materials overcomes the need for such frequent watering.

In most soils, where drainage is not stopped by hard-pan, there is very little lateral movement of water. A 6-inch-wide ditch will moisten a little more than a 9-inch strip of soil. Of course the more water and the longer it is applied, the greater the lateral movement. But don't count on a spread of water much wider than the area to which it is applied.

USE SOIL SAMPLING TUBE to check water penetration, take samples for soil analysis. Compacted surface layer (A); damp soil (B) to ring finger; dry soil (C) for last few inches. Overall tube length is 12 inches.

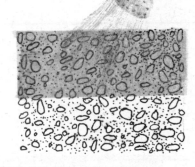

ONE GALLON OF WATER may thoroughly water a given volume of soil; one-half gallon will not "lightly water" the same volume but will water only one half of it.

Making Compost...
the How and Why

Composting—utilizing otherwise "waste" materials to provide organic soil conditioning, material for mulching, and for potting mixes—is one of the oldest of all gardening practices. On most uncultivated lands, composting is a natural process: Leaves, grasses, and animal remains gradually decompose through the combined efforts of microorganisms and weather. Directions in this chapter tell you how to accelerate these natural processes to produce quantities of compost in a relatively short time.

Composting: Pro

If you add raw organic materials with a high carbon/nitrogen ratio (see page 10) to the soil, they will temporarily tie up the soil's available nitrogen during initial decomposition stages. But these same carbon-rich, nitrogen-poor materials will decompose in a compost heap without adversely affecting, even temporarily, the soil's nitrogen supply.

If you add green or dried materials directly to soil, the nutrients released during initial decomposition may be leached out of the root zone before the soil is ready for planting. In a well-managed compost heap, however, you apply only enough water to moisten the composting materials. Then, little or no runoff will occur which could carry away valuable nutrients.

You don't have to take up much valuable garden space to have a compost operation. See the diagram on page 37 for dimensions of an ideal 3-chamber arrangement suitable for a suburban garden. A double-chamber or single heap will occupy even less space. Put your compost operation in an area which is not readily visible or which may not be suited for growing plants. But be sure to locate it near a water source so that you can moisten it if materials become too dry.

Composting: Con

There are two potential drawbacks to composting: bad odors and flies. Make no mistake about it, you can expect to have some of both unless you are an exceptionally knowledgeable and careful gardener (and lucky, too).

Two types of bacteria can decompose organic matter. *Aerobic* bacteria operate in the presence of air, moisture, and high temperature; their work is relatively odorless and rapid. The other bacteria of decomposition are the *anaerobic* types which thrive in a moist but airless environment and under cooler conditions. These are the offensive-smelling bacteria which have given composting a bad reputation. To prevent their appearance and growth, turn the materials in your heap as often as is necessary to keep it well-aerated and odorless (see "Turning", page 42).

Flies will be a problem if you fill your heap with high-protein (nitrogen) materials and then neglect it. Piles of unturned grass clippings offer attractive breeding-places for flies. Animal wastes of all kinds—from table scraps to excrement—amount to an invitation to flies. In addition, meat scraps will attract other animals—domestic and wild.

THE COMPOSTING IDEA...AT-A-GLANCE

This compost setup combines several features which operate together to make compost quickly and easily. Less elaborate setups will also make compost effectively but may be more trouble to manage and the results may be slower in coming.

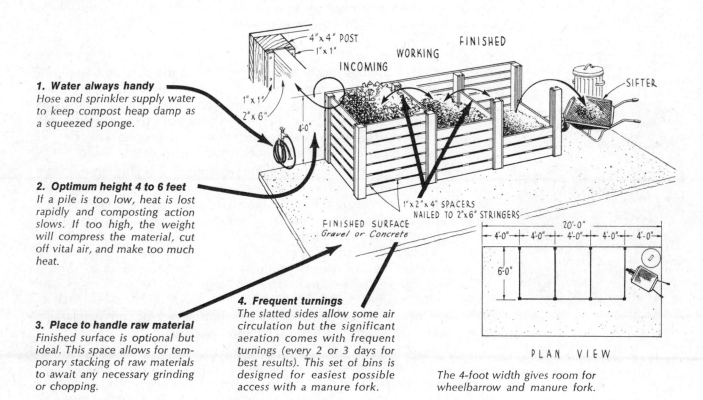

1. Water always handy
Hose and sprinkler supply water to keep compost heap damp as a squeezed sponge.

2. Optimum height 4 to 6 feet
If a pile is too low, heat is lost rapidly and composting action slows. If too high, the weight will compress the material, cut off vital air, and make too much heat.

3. Place to handle raw material
Finished surface is optional but ideal. This space allows for temporary stacking of raw materials to await any necessary grinding or chopping.

4. Frequent turnings
The slatted sides allow some air circulation but the significant aeration comes with frequent turnings (every 2 or 3 days for best results). This set of bins is designed for easiest possible access with a manure fork.

The 4-foot width gives room for wheelbarrow and manure fork.

HOW TO MAKE COMPOST

The "classic" compost pile is made like this: On bare earth, place a 6-inch layer of plant remains from the garden and kitchen (leaves, weeds, sawdust, etc.); cover this with a 3-inch layer of manure, and on top of the manure add a thin sprinkling of topsoil; rock powders, wood ashes, or lime may be added to this, if desired, to amplify the nutrient content of the finished product. Water these materials enough to moisten—but not saturate—them, then follow the same layering procedure until the pile is 4-6 feet high. Finally, apply a coating of topsoil to the heap to seal in moisture, punch holes in the seal for ventilation—from the crown straight down to the earth below—about every 3 feet. (An easier method for making the ventilation shafts is to build up the heap around poles, then remove them when the heap is completed.) Turn the heap after about 3 weeks and again in about 2 weeks following the first turn; compost should be ready to use approximately 3 months after the heap is built.

While many gardeners still successfully prepare compost according to the method above, more recent experience has revealed ways which are quicker and often less work. The layers of plant wastes, manure, and soil may actually impede aeration—and thereby slow the decomposition process—since layers of relatively homogeneous materials will tend to pack down. Depending upon the materials used and the amount of moisture in the heap, you may have to turn the pile more frequently to prevent the proliferation of anaerobic bacteria.

Regardless of the materials you use, the success of your compost operation depends upon the five points that follow. If you understand these you can get your compost heap off to a good start—and you should be able to counteract most problems that might arise.

Texture of raw materials. Up to a point, the smaller the particle size of raw materials the faster decomposition will take place. More surfaces are available for decay bacteria to attack when organic particles are small. If the consistency of your materials is *too* fine, however, your pile will settle into a solid, airless mass. To hasten the decomposition process you can, of course, break up leaves, twigs, and other organic materials by hand.

For the conscientious composter there are a number of grinders available especially designed to cut or shred organic matter into particles small enough to decompose rapidly. All models operate on gasoline-powered motors, although some brands also offer you the choice of an electric power source. If you choose an electric grinder, be sure you have a heavy duty electrical circuit; with anything weaker you will repeatedly blow fuses or trip your circuit breaker. Electric grinders generally have about a 1-horsepower motor; the gasoline-powered motors range from 3½ to 6-horsepower. Prices of the most widely sold machines will range from about $150 to slightly less than $400. Larger models are manufactured for commercial use, their prices ranging up into the thousands of dollars.

With a grinder, you will be able to compost nearly all organic materials from the garden—rose and tree prunings, berry vines, pits, tough stalks, leaves—plus vegetable kitchen wastes as well. Grinding, however, should not be so fine as to cause pulping of succulent material. Grinders available for home use are capable of handling branches only up to about 1½ inches in diameter.

FAMILIAR AUTUMN SIGHT in areas where deciduous trees are grown are the annual piles of burning leaves; if composted, instead, they would be ready to enrich the soil by the following spring or summer.

TO VENTILATE COMPOST HEAP, punch holes with a pole through the heap to the earth below.

GARDEN REFUSE (such as cornstalks, shown here) is easily converted by grinder into small particles which decompose rapidly.

COMPOST GRINDER did this to apricot prunings (top), spent annuals (bottom).

PILE OF APRICOT PRUNINGS identical to one at left (6 by 10 by 4 feet high) was reduced by compost grinder into 4 by 4 by 1½-foot pile at right.

Height and Heat. Heat build-up is all-important in composting, and one factor which determines how high the temperature goes is the height of the pile. Too shallow a pile loses heat rapidly because there isn't enough material above the heat source to insulate it and prevent loss. Below-optimum temperatures mean that heat-loving bacteria, working at the center of the pile, won't flourish as they should; therefore, composting will take a longer time.

Too high a pile, on the other hand, means that material will be compressed by its own weight; this may produce too much heat plus a shortage of air at the bottom. Too much heat tends to kill off desirable bacteria, and the lack of air encourages the foul-smelling anaerobic types.

A height of 4 to 6 feet will satisfy the heat-retention and aeration requirements. As decomposition progresses, the materials in a 5-foot heap will shrink in volume to perhaps 3 or 3½ feet.

In all but the most severe climates, outdoor air temperatures won't affect heat build-up in a pile of proper dimensions, so composting can be done in winter.

Nitrogen. The pile with too little nitrogen (needed by the decay-producing bacteria to grow and multiply) will not generate enough heat to compost the materials rapidly. Instead, because of its high carbon/nitrogen ratio, this pile will decay gradually through action of cool-temperature organisms—largely fungi.

This means that if you're composting tough materials like dry or woody weeds, ivy trimmings, or prunings—all with high C/N ratios—you should mix succulent material like lawn clippings and soft, leafy wastes into the pile for an easily-decomposed source of nitrogen. If you have no nitrogenous green materials, you can add nitrogen in the form of organic fertilizers.

COVER FOR COMPOST pile may be necessary in periods of heavy rainfall to prevent pile from becoming waterlogged and losing good aeration.

Moisture. Although the compost pile should always be moist, it should never be soggy, since excess water limits the air supply. The wetter the pile becomes, the more frequently you'll have to turn it to keep aerobic bacteria flourishing (see "Turning", page 42).

Green refuse usually needs no additional water at all in the beginning, but you should wet down dry stalks and grass as you build the pile. Moisture of the pile as a whole should run between 40 to 60 per cent—about as wet as a squeezed sponge.

The pile will steam as heat begins to build; at this time it may become dry at the center. If this happens, the rapid decomposition process stops abruptly. During this period, occasionally insert a pole into the pile and pull it out to test for heat and moisture. If the pole comes out moist, warm, and with no trace of foul odor your heap is functioning normally.

In dry climates you may have to water your pile every 4 or 5 days, but in areas where rainfall is heavy you will need to take precautions to keep the pile from becoming soggy. A rounded pile tends to shed water like a thatched roof, but if rains are continuous, a covering—polyethylene plastic, a tarpaulin, or even a wooden roof—will divert excess moisture. If the pile does become water-logged and anaerobic bacteria threaten to take over, daily turning will put it back into a healthy condition.

SIMPLE BIN—PORTABLE AND COLLAPSIBLE

The bin pictured below is a very satisfactory home-garden compost factory. It is constructed of 1 by 2-inch redwood and strips of lath, with poultry wire sandwiched between the pieces of wood (all poultry wire is galvanized to resist rusting). The wire mesh sides allow good ventilation so air can circulate freely. There are two L-shaped sides held together with screw hooks and eyes. It holds exactly a cubic yard.

The designer of this compost bin begins making his compost in early spring, filling it with alternate layers of garden refuse and vegetable kitchen wastes. On every second or third 4-inch layer he sprinkles blood meal; nitrogen in the blood meal helps speed the process of decay by nourishing the bacteria that are involved in decomposing the raw materials. When the bin is full, he seals the pile with a thin layer of soil on the top and wets the pile down.

The pile can be turned over by removing the sides of the bin, setting them up next to the pile that is left standing, and then forking the pile back into the bin, upside down.

HOOKS AND EYES hold sides of this portable bin together; sides may be unhooked for reassembly in new location.

GOOD VENTILATION of the compost heap is provided by the wire mesh sides; sturdy 1 by 2-inch lumber frames keep the sides rigid.

Turning. Three purposes are served by turning the compost pile. During the first few weeks of initial decomposition the pile begins to pack down and loses some of the aeration necessary for the aerobic process. When you turn the pile, you loosen the materials and introduce more air. If your pile is too soggy, turning will introduce air to dry the materials somewhat, preventing a takeover by anaerobic bacteria.

Finally, turning provides the opportunity to rearrange the decaying material. This brings the outer, less decomposed portions of the pile into the center where the high heat bacteria will again go to work. The pile will heat up again, but more briefly. When it cools, the decomposition process is finished and the compost is ready for you to use.

U.C. Quick Compost

The University of California developed a set of procedures that can produce usable compost in 2-3 weeks. You may not be able to meet all the conditions necessary for such speedy results, but you can produce compost fairly quickly by employing the UC principles.

The steps to success with the University of California quick compost are not difficult to follow, but you must observe them closely if you are to achieve a usable product in a few weeks. The most important point to remember is the texture of raw materials you are going to compost: Grind or chop them so that they are approximately an inch or less in diameter. The finely chopped materials offer more surface area to the decomposition bacteria than do unchopped materials, so that decomposition is able to take place much more rapidly. The second really critical point is that the pile must be turned every 2 or 3 days. The frequent turning insures good aeration so that the microorganisms can work efficiently. Best results follow when the raw materials have a carbon nitrogen ratio of about 30/1 (see page 10). Finally, as with any compost pile, the best height is between 4 and 6 feet, while the moisture content should be kept at about that of a squeezed-out sponge.

BASIC COMPOST PILE is single heap of organic materials which is turned in place. Here, railroad ties contain the operation, help maintain more even temperature at edges of pile.

Sheet Composting and Green Manuring

If you have enough land that you can afford to take a portion out of cultivation for several months, you can improve your soil with organic materials by sheet composting, green manuring, or a combination of the two.

For sheet composting you spread raw organic materials over the soil you wish to improve and then dig them in. The decomposition takes place in the soil. Autumn is a convenient season to do this, as there is then usually an abundance of organic "waste" material. Especially if you dig in organic matter that has a high carbon content, fall is advantageous: The nitrogen used by soil bacteria to decompose it will be temporarily tied up by the bacteria during the months of winter rain or snow, so will not be leached away; nitrogen will be released again, after much decomposition has taken place, in spring when the soil and season are right for planting.

SHEET COMPOSTING is done by spading fallen leaves, grass clippings, other non-woody garden refuse into the soil.

Green manuring consists of raising a crop (usually a grass or a legume) until it reaches near-maturity—then you dig it into the soil. The green crop has a higher nitrogen content than do dried materials and also decomposes more rapidly so that often you can replant within a month of its return to the soil.

If you are starting with soil that is low in both fertility and organic matter you can sow several successive green manure crops; each one will materially improve the soil. In poor soils the first few green manure crops are usually grasses (rye, for example) which will grow where fertility and soil structure are poor. When these conditions improve, a sowing of a nitrogen-fixing legume (such as alfalfa or clover) will further increase the soil fertility when added to the soil. Check with your county agricultural extension service for the green manure crops best adapted to your climate and soil.

The two processes—sheet composting and green manuring—can be combined in one operation. This is particularly useful when your materials for sheet composting have a high carbon/nitrogen ratio (see page 10). The nitrogen from the green manure (and especially from legumes) will be available to meet the bacterial demands for breaking down the dry materials. The materials for sheet composting may be spread over the green manure crop and the two then simultaneously dug into the soil.

How to Foil Plant Eaters and Plant Spoilers

In past years, some gardeners have had the mistaken understanding that they must spray regularly, frequently, and on a large scale basis if they want an attractive and pleasant garden. This is not true. Massive use of insecticides in gardens just doesn't make sense. Beneficial insects are killed along with the real pests; ecological balance of the garden is thrown out of kilter; some pests may reappear and assume greater importance than nature would normally allow.

Still, rare is the gardener who has not had to spray infested plants from time-to-time. Spraying can make sense when pests are not being controlled by natural predators, and when common-sense measures (such as plant washing with a hose) don't do the job.

It is important to remember these things: 1) Spray only the host plant or plants; and 2) Use the right spray for the pest you are trying to eradicate (see the chart on page 50).

Many gardeners make it a practice to apply a dormant spray—such as lime sulfur or oil—on trees and shrubs in winter when they are leafless. Such sprays will get rid of pests spending the winter on the plants, and will also prevent some diseases.

CONTROL MEASURES

Your first step toward maintaining a harmonious garden balance is to recognize the value of a number of natural predators that can help you. These are discussed on pages 46-47.

Weather plays a huge—and often unheralded—part in regulating insect populations. Many insects migrate annually. Certain specific changes in temperature or day-length trigger their instinct to move on to a different kind of province at a certain time. Other insects are triggered by climate or weather change to go quickly into a stage of dormancy or inactivity in which they are harmless. Often, man has intervened into nature's affairs with a spray gun just in advance of a weather change that in itself accomplished the result he desired. Then, with the disappearance of the insects, the spray got credit for an accomplishment that was nature's.

Some insects are plagued by their own diseases which become fatal in time. This explains, for example, the sudden, overnight death of a colony of tent caterpillars on a tree branch in your yard.

Healthy, vigorous plants and a clean garden are the best forms of preventive maintenance. A strong, actively growing plant can fend off insects and disease far better than a struggling, undernourished one.

The following 9-point program should help you to keep your garden relatively free from pests.

1. First line of defense is careful planning. Many plant troubles blamed on diseases or insects are really caused by poor soil drainage. See page 8 for ways to make soil contain more oxygen (that's what "good drainage" means). Growing plants in raised beds and containers is another way to give them good drainage.

Mix plants together as much as possible. Large expanses of just one kind of plant invite attacks by the organisms that thrive on that plant. Furthermore, that one kind of plant probably cannot offer sustenance to the organisms that would kill the plant's pests. In other words, mixed plantings do much to bring about a natural balance in which organisms keep each other in check.

Rotate annual plants, especially vegetables. Alternate between leaf and root crops. Some vegetables—notably tomatoes and beans—should not be grown in the same place year after year. All of this avoids reinfestation by insects or diseases that can live over in the soil from one year to the next.

Allow for adequate air circulation around plants known to get mildew.

2. Keep the ground surface clean. Compost or dig in all fallen leaves and fruit. Do the same with soft, decayable mulches that have been in place for longer than one or two seasons. Layers of debris that stay in place for a long time become breeding or hiding places for insects and diseases. Do not put diseased or insect-infested plants or plant parts on the compost heap. They may spread the problem.

3. Learn to know your enemy. Get a hand lens and examine stems, leaf surfaces, and fruit surfaces to see what is eating or discoloring them. Look for tiny eggs, tiny puncture holes, excrement, cast-off skins, stationary insects—all of these signs become clues to what is happening. After a while you may be able to stop an infestation in its early stage or deduce that pests aren't causing the trouble at all.

4. Use commando tactics. This advice is self-evident. The fastest and most satisfactory way to get rid of a creature that is eating or damaging a plant is to pick him off, drop him, and squash him (or administer the *coup de grace* however you wish). This works easily for large and slow-moving daytime creatures. It also will work for some nighttime creatures such as snails, slugs, and cutworms, but you have to go out at night with a flashlight to find them.

Tiny creatures and those that move or fly fast and those that feed in tree tops may have to be dealt with in some other way. First, try washing them off with water from a hose. Only a few individuals of a few species will have the strength and determination to crawl or fly from the group back to the plant. Most will starve, die of exposure, or get eaten by predators. If the washed-off insects recur in equal or greater numbers, you may have to spray (see point 6 on page 48 and the chart on page 50).

UNDERGROUND PESTS like gophers and moles will be foiled by chicken wire bottom of this raised bed, yet plant roots are not confined.

In California where summers are rainless, washing mites off also washes off the dust layer in which the mites hide. That dust layer seems essential to mites' continued damage.

An old toothbrush is a useful weapon for commando gardeners. Dip it in oil spray to brush off scale insects, mealybugs, and other determined creatures that won't be knocked off or discouraged in any other way. Sometimes you can use a cotton swab the same way.

5. Use and encourage natural controls. Under the heading "natural controls" come all the insect predators—from toads to birds to ladybugs to diseases that kill insects.

You can buy some beneficial insects (ladybugs, praying mantises, lacewings, and trichogramma wasps) and release them in your garden. However, this is no guarantee of success. Perhaps your garden conditions will not be to their liking, providing little incentive for them to remain in your area. Or they may leave soon after release because day-length or temperature tells them it's time to migrate. (That often happens with ladybugs.) But some gardeners have found that such insects can and will do a measurable job of eating insects.

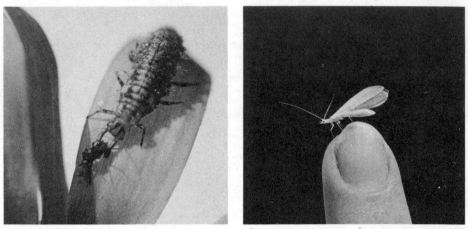

LACEWING LARVA grabs aphid (left), sucks juice from aphid until only a body hull is left (center). Adult lacewing is shown at right.

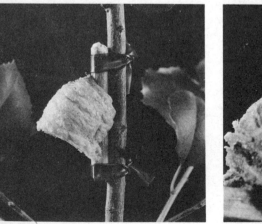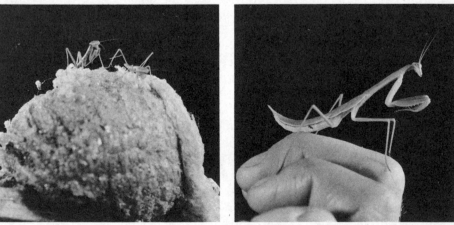

PRAYING MANTIS egg case is attached to sturdy plant stem (left). Baby mantises (center) emerge from case, mature to adult at right.

Birds have a reputation for keeping down insect populations in home gardens. Actually, not all birds eat insects. Some eat only seeds; others eat both seeds and insects. Bird books and Audubon Society offices can supply you with plans for birdhouses that will attract certain species. Among the species that are known to eat insects are: titmice, chickadees, verdins, bushtits, and nuthatches; mockingbirds and thrashers; thrushes (including robins and bluebirds); wrens, waxwings, shrikes, gnatcatchers and kinglets, warblers, and orioles.

Almost all birds—insect eaters included—seem to enjoy and be attracted to bird baths. In the line of feed, the best way to attract the insect eaters is to put up suet in convenient spots for the birds. The easiest method is to simply bind a lump of suet to a tree branch with cotton cord. For small birds, hang a suet lump from a string; that way large birds can only peck at it as they fly by. You can also hang suet in a loosely woven net bag or even melt it down and pour it into a hollowed-out coconut or similar receptacle. (For a suet substitute in a coconut, try peanut butter.) Suet encaged in large mesh chicken wire sometimes may not be a good idea: Some birds, in their eagerness to eat, can damage their beaks on the wire.

SUET (in mesh) attract birds to feeder at left; seeds in melted suet go into center feeder; seeds alone feed birds at right.

PINE CONE soaked in suet (left) attracts insect eaters; tray of seeds (center) and bird bath (right) lure variety of birds.

Another way to attract birds of all kinds (including bug eaters) to a garden is to grow plenty of plants that are bushy to the ground and plants that form edible (to birds) berries and fruits.

Although less attractive, frogs, toads, lizards, salamanders, and snakes also pay their way in the numbers of insects they consume. Frogs, of course, require water to live. Toads are easier to keep—they ask nothing from you except that you look where you are stepping.

Domestic birds you keep as pets will eat anything they see moving. Ducks are especially fond of snails and slugs; turn over a few boards where snails are hiding and the ducks will get the idea. Keep ducks away from succulents and other juicy plants: They'll eat them. Chickens (bantam or standard sized) love little insects and newly sprouted weeds, but keep the birds confined or they'll eat garden plants right along with the weeds. A trained Chinese goose can weed orchards or any place where plants are tall so the goose feet can't squash them. All these birds feed mainly in the early morning and late evening, so let them wander at those times.

Another control method for certain damaging insects is spray preparations that contain organisms of specific diseases which will kill the insect larvae. (Not all of these products are readily available to home gardeners.) Milky spore disease that kills grubs of the Japanese beetle (eastern U.S.) offers the greatest effectiveness for the least effort in combating this pest. Infected individual insects can spread the disease to healthy individuals, and the disease will live in the soil to attack grubs which hatch during the following year. Another such biological control is *Bacillus thuringiensis* which will kill larvae of certain moths and butterflies—most notably those of the oak moth. It works by paralyzing the larvae's intestines.

6. Use toxic materials only when you must. Under some circumstances you may have to use certain simple toxic materials to kill damaging insects or mites. One such circumstance is if you try squirting the insects with a jet of water and they just hang on, grinning at you. Another is if you can't see or find the insect that's eating the holes or the scallops in the leaves.

If the persistent hangers-on are aphids (soft, round, in colonies), scale insects (hard, flattish, immobile), or mealybugs (immobile, flattish, waxy white) there are two materials to try next. One is soapy water applied with a tank sprayer. Mix nine level tablespoons (or about two ounces) of soap flakes, not detergent, in three gallons of water.

The other choice is oil spray. If you follow label instructions, it is an absolutely safe, non-poisonous, non-polluting product quite similar to medicinal mineral oil and it is quite effective. The oil kills the immobile and slow-moving insects by smothering them, but the oil film is invisible to you.

Tree-climbing pests can be thwarted by using any of several manufactured adhesive barriers. You spread the sticky substance around the bases of tree trunks to prevent insects from crawling up. It is especially valuable in keeping out aphids (by way of keeping out the ants that bring them), cutworms, beetles, and snails.

For hundreds of years, gardeners have used sulfur to kill mites, prevent mildew, and to control other fungus diseases. You have a choice of a dust or a wettable powder (for liquid spray), but when the temperature rises above 85° there is a danger of damage to foliage. Follow closely the directions and cautions on the label.

Lime sulfur spray is a safe, simple compound with a long history of successful use. Alone or with oil spray it can be an all-purpose midwinter cleanup spray. Or, you can use it according to label instructions during the growing season to combat mites and several diseases.

Bordeaux solution, like lime sulfur, is an old-time manufactured (but basically simple) compound. Applied at the right time in the right way it can destroy many plant disease organisms and even repel some insects. Bordeaux solution (and its components) has never been indicted for any kind of environmental pollution.

Botanical sprays—those which have been derived from plants—fall into two categories. Some are actually toxic to insects; others are simply offensive to them and discourage their presence. The most common toxic botanicals are pyrethrum, rotenone, and ryania; these are sold (the first two generally in combination) ready to be diluted and used in the garden. The second group of botanicals consists of the home-made extracts from juices of such plants as onion, garlic, pepper, marigold—almost anything having a strong and often unpleasant odor. General directions for preparing these sprays are found on page 48.

HOME-MADE SPRAY preparation is measured, added to water (left), then put into small hand sprayer for use only on infested plant.

7. Spray only the infested plants. And use only enough spray to cover the target plant. By spraying no more than the pest-ridden plant you minimize the danger of killing other life forms that are harmless or helpful.

The best device for doing this is a tank-type pressure sprayer. Use only the amount of spray you need to do the job at hand, and wet only the plant that has the pests, nothing else. If you use a hose-end sprayer, keep in mind that most kinds put out about twice as much material (per unit of time) as a pressure sprayer. So, with a hose-end you'll need to move along more quickly in order not to spray needlessly the ground and surrounding plants.

8. Don't demand (or even expect) total eradication of the problem. A certain amount of pest damage is inevitable, and to attempt complete control is to endanger needlessly the harmless life forms in and even beyond your garden. In a reasonably balanced garden situation, the damage done by insect pests will be insignificant—and your enjoyment of the plants should not be diminished because of a few holes or puckers in the leaves, flowers, or fruits.

Food crops are the one exception: They require a close watch for insect damage. Even so, you can sacrifice a small percentage of your fruits and vegetables to pests without materially affecting your harvest—and at a great saving of the time and effort you would have to spend toward total eradication.

WHICH CONTROL FOR WHICH PEST?

Pests	Pyrethrum	Rotenone (cube)	Ryania	Soap Solution	Lime Sulfur	Dusting Sulfur	Sabadilla	Petroleum Oils	Metaldehyde	Hand Methods	Adhesive Barriers	Bacillus thuringiensis	Milky Spore Disease
Leaf Chewers													
Beetles	•	•	•							•	•		
Japanese beetle			•							•			•
Weevils										•			
Caterpillars	•	•								•	•		
Grasshoppers							•			•			
Oak moths										•		•	
Snails and slugs									•	•			
Sucking Insects													
Aphids	•	•	•	•			•	•		•			
Leafhoppers	•	•	•										
Mealybugs								•					
Scale					•			•		•			
Spider mites			•	•	•	•		•					
Spittlebugs		•											
Thrips	•	•	•					•					
Whiteflies	•	•						•					
Soil Pests													
Cutworms										•			
Grubs										•			
Lawn moths	•	•								•			
Burrowers													
Codling moths			•					•		•			
Leaf miners		•								•			
Corn earworms			•							•			
Borers										•	•		
Nuisance Insects													
Ants										•	•		

9. Get rid of the weak or susceptible plants. If an insect or disease problem persists, and if the plants involved are not essential to your physical or emotional well-being: Remove them from your garden and replace them with plants that will be less susceptible to repeated problems. There are hundreds of garden plants that are never, rarely, or not significantly bothered by pests of any kind.

It surprises some people to learn that native North American plants get the most pests, generally speaking, and exotics from far places such as Australia and India get the fewest. Our native plants support our native insects, mites, and fungus life. The pest-free exotic plants were brought here by seed, not as living plants, and hence they left *their* native pests in their native continents.

More and more, modern plant breeding is aimed toward production of varieties and strains which will resist common disease organisms. Now you have the opportunity to buy and plant such disease-resistant plants as rust-resistant snapdragons, virus-resistant tomatoes, and mildew-resistant roses, for example. It makes good sense to use these plants.

NEMATODE PROBLEM? TRY MARIGOLDS

Of interest to organic gardeners is the research which has discovered that marigolds will reduce or even eliminate nematodes within a 3-foot radius of the plant. Worldwide in distribution, nematodes are tiny worms, some species of which infect animals and man while others prefer plants. The microscopic soil nematodes can injure plants in two ways: Directly, their feeding on plant roots can cause stunting and wilting; indirectly, their puncture wounds can let in damaging fungi or bacteria. They are a major agricultural problem (especially in lighter, sandier soils) and a headache for some home gardeners as well.

How do marigolds affect nematodes? All plants give off chemicals called "root diffusates." Nematodes sense these substances in order to locate and zero in on a host plant. However, root diffusates from some non-host plants actually can mask or neutralize those from a host plant, thereby throwing the nematodes off the track. If they are produced in sufficient quantities (as in the case of marigolds), these diffusates even can be toxic to nematodes.

In test plots that contained marigolds, researchers found as many as 90 per cent fewer nematodes than in test plots without marigolds. The plants do not give this degree of control consistently, but all marigolds will suppress the worms to some extent.

Many gardeners traditionally have planted marigolds in the belief that they keep away various harmful insects, especially aphids. So far there is no documented proof or disproof of this, but there is some evidence that marigolds can reduce the number of certain weeds around them.

Before you plant quantities of marigolds just for nematode control, be sure that nematodes are a significant problem in your garden. Root-knot nematodes (the most common kind) produce nodules or swellings on plant roots; but remember that roots of many legumes—members of the pea and bean family—will have root nodules of nitrogen-fixing bacteria. For above-ground indications of possible nematode trouble, look for plants that are strangely susceptible to bacterial wilts, fungus, or root rots.

Marigolds come in large and small forms, can be attractive when grouped together or when scattered throughout garden for nematode control. Colors range from nearly white through yellow and orange to dark red.

Solving Lawn Problems

Some lawn grasses are regularly beset by fungus diseases. The bent grasses are especially susceptible and bluegrass sometimes may be affected (the latter gets rust badly). The only way to control lawn diseases is to spray or treat regularly with strong manufactured fungicides. If you want a lawn that won't demand fungicides, grow Bermuda grasses in the warmer southern latitudes or a bluegrass-fescue combination in the northern latitudes. Even then, expect some grief with bluegrass—rust.

Lawns do not suffer from "lawn moth" or "sod webworm" or "grubs" as much as some literature would have you believe. Moths flit over lawns at dusk in summer as a matter of routine. This flitting does not necessarily mean that damage will follow or that spraying will be necessary. Brown spots on lawns are more often caused by fungus (see above), drought, or lack of fertilizer. In the event that you find your lawn really is being damaged by the chewing of sod webworms there is one manufactured product you can use—pyrethrum. It is fairly effective against sod webworm, and it has no adverse effect on the environment. White grubs are found in small isolated colonies, and the affected lawn area is typically no larger than a doormat in size. It takes only a few minutes to roll back the small section of lawn and hand-pick the grubs for destruction.

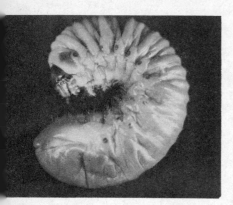 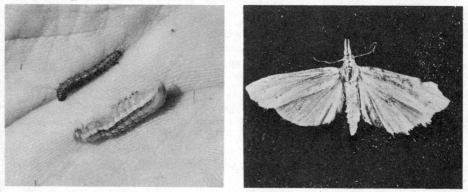

LAWN PESTS include shrimp-like white grubs (left) and sod webworm (center) which are larvae for lawn moths (right).

How to Control Weeds

The time-honored methods for ridding your garden of weeds are hoeing (see arsenal of hoes on facing page) and pulling by hand; the latter is preferable when working in lawns or close to valuable plants.

Controlling weeds in gravel, paths, driveways, or vacant lots is a special problem. Lightweight weed oil does a very effective job—it is safe to use, isn't sticky, and won't permanently stain sidewalks or patios. It will create a strong odor for a few days, but that soon disappears. The younger the weeds, the less oil you need, but each weed must be thoroughly wetted. Tank sprayers are the most satisfactory method of applying the spray. Use the tank under low pressure (25 to 30 pounds) and keep the nozzle close to the ground to avoid making a fog that would drift. Walk backwards as

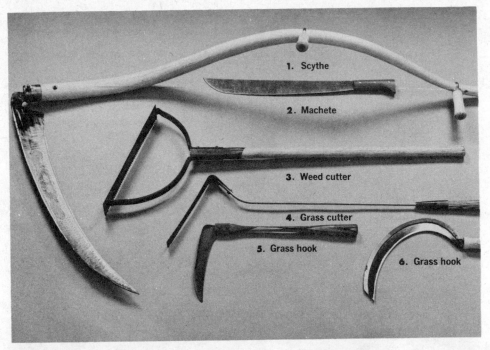

1. Scythe

2. Machete

3. Weed cutter

4. Grass cutter

5. Grass hook

6. Grass hook

WEED CONTROL BY HAND may be accomplished in various ways. Cutting tools (top left) can reduce tall weeds to stubble, good for composting or green manuring; hoes (bottom left and right) will chop weeds out (numbers 7-12), also make furrows for planting (numbers 10 and 11), cut off weeds as they pass between blades (number 13), or slide beneath the soil surface to cut roots (numbers 14-17).

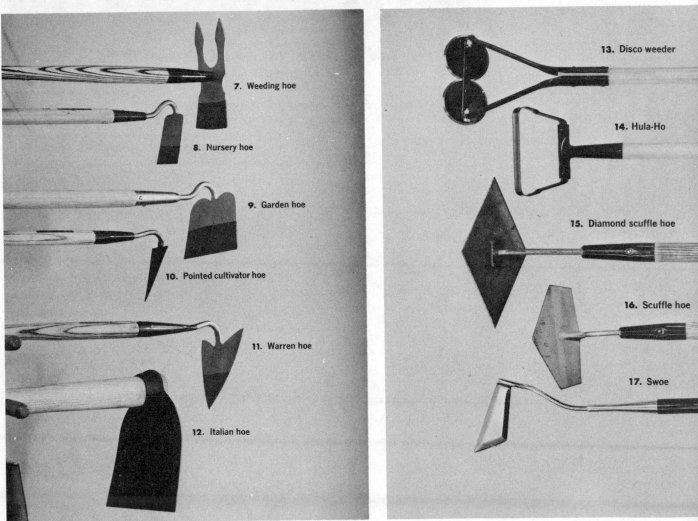

7. Weeding hoe

8. Nursery hoe

9. Garden hoe

10. Pointed cultivator hoe

11. Warren hoe

12. Italian hoe

13. Disco weeder

14. Hula-Ho

15. Diamond scuffle hoe

16. Scuffle hoe

17. Swoe

you spray so you won't be walking through the oil. Oil sprays will kill only the top growth, so you may have to spray again to get strongly rooted perennials.

Your best method for *preventing* germination of weed seeds and growth of weeds is to use plastic film or thick layers of straw (or similar material) as a soil-covering mulch between plants you want to keep (see pages 30-32).

PLASTIC FILM over soil surface prevents weeds from growing among your garden plants and also serves as a mulch.

Bees...Most Gardens Need Them

Many people carefully avoid bees—and even try to banish them from their gardens—because they fear that a bee's primary function is to sting. However, their value to the gardener who raises fruits and various vegetables should be obvious.

Besides producing honey and beeswax, most bees pollinate flowers. Citrus and deciduous fruit trees, for example, need bees to carry pollen from flower to flower and thereby make fruit set. Some deciduous fruits (notably peaches and apricots) will set fruit with little help from bees, but others (such as apples, pears, and cherries) depend upon bees for pollination. Cantaloupes, watermelons, cucumbers, squash, and berries also benefit from the activities of bees.

If you have many fruit trees or if you grow a crop that is aided by bees, you might consider keeping a beehive. The bees will help pollinate your crops, and you can have their honey. In addition, you will have the enjoyment of watching the bees and their cooperative society.

The common honey-bee is just one of many species in the large family Apoidea and the one you see most often, buzzing from flower to flower. Among the less-frequently observed kinds are the burrowing bees, carpenter bees, leaf-cutting bees, sweat bees, and (of course) bumblebees. All are beneficial to the gardener.

Even the "safest" of sprays can be poisonous to bees. If you spray *after* plants finish blooming there is no danger that bees may be on them in any quantity. Because bees gather pollen (which is a powder), liquid sprays are safer than powder forms.

How to Grow Vegetables

ARTICHOKE

The artichoke is a fine ornamental plant as well as food producer. As a vegetable it grows best where summers are cool and moist. Roots are deep, fleshy, and perennial so prepare soil thoroughly and deeply with much organic material. Artichokes must have good drainage, so plant in raised beds if really heavy soil or hardpan is a problem. Plant dormant roots (or plants from containers) in winter or early spring; set the root shanks vertically with growth buds or shoots just above soil level, spacing plants 4 to 6 feet apart. If only seeds are available, you can sow them where you want the plants to grow; place several seeds together and cover with an inch of screened compost or light soil. When they grow to several inches, thin to one plant.

For vegetable production, artichokes must not have their growth checked—which means that plant roots always need to be moist. Water thoroughly once a week (or more often, if necessary) wetting the entire root system. Watch for aphids, but use only a soap solution or blast them off with water after buds have formed (if you're growing them for eating). Harvest buds while they are still tight and plump. At end of season, cut off old stalks near ground level when leaves begin to yellow. In cold-winter areas, cut tops of plants to 12 inches in fall, tie them over the root crown, and mulch heavily. When the plant sprouts again in spring, remove all but three of the strongest shoots if you grow them for food. About every 5 years, dig and divide the root crowns and replant in freshly prepared soil.

If coarser grades of bone meal and a rock phosphate are worked into the root zone at planting time, artichokes will only need a nitrogen fertilizer yearly until you divide and replant them. Use cottonseed meal if your soil or water is alkaline; otherwise choose from the nitrogen sources listed on page 15. In mild-climate areas, apply this between the time you harvest the last buds and the start of new growth. In cold-winter areas, fertilize in spring after danger of frost is past. Artichokes are heavy feeders, so may benefit from another application during the growing season.

ASPARAGUS

The main edible crop is produced in spring to early summer, before hottest weather arrives; after that the plants can be a fairly attractive ornamental. In mild climates, planting is done in fall or winter; plant in early spring where weather is cold. Finest results will come from soils that have been previously double dug or at least spaded deeply, as asparagus roots are planted deep. To plant, dig a trench at least a foot wide and deep, and long enough to accommodate the number of roots you have when planted 18 inches apart; do this about 2 weeks before you intend to plant. Work about 6 inches of manure, or manure and compost or sludge, into the soil at the bottom of the trench; also include a generous sprinkling of bone meal and a rock potash into this soil, as roots remain in place for many years. Then soak thoroughly. Set out the roots in the trench so that tops are about 8 inches below the soil surface, and spread out roots evenly. Cover with 2 inches of soil and water again; leave the remaining soil alongside the trench. Gradually add this soil evenly throughout the trench as the asparagus tips grow upward, filling in until just the tips are exposed. When the trench is filled, let the plants grow without cutting.

Soak soil deeply whenever it begins to dry out. Roots are deep but must not lack moisture. Don't harvest any spears the first year; the object at that time is to build up a strong root mass and plants need the foliage to do this. During the second spring you can begin harvesting spears but only for 4–6 weeks or until thin spears appear to indicate roots need building up.

Fertilize, and let plants grow until foliage dies down. From the third year on (asparagus plantings will produce well for 10 years and more) you can cut spears until about early summer. Cut them at ground level when they are 5–8 inches long. In cold-winter climates mulch the plantings before frosts arrive and let dead stems remain to catch snow which will also act as insulation for the roots. Control asparagus beetle (should it appear) with rotenone.

In early spring, fertilize with an organic nitrogen material, preferably one that will also contain some phosphorus or potash such as fish meal or cottonseed meal (if your soil is not acid). Mulch with well-rotted manure or compost which will serve as very weak fertilizers and will moderate soil temperatures. Fertilize again in summer after you quit cutting spears.

BEANS

Beans are a warm-weather crop and won't begin to grow until the soil warms up. Prepare soil as described on page 23 under "Annuals and Vegetables." Sow seeds in place—an inch deep and about 3 inches apart in rows 2-3 feet apart.

If seeds haven't sprouted in 2 weeks they may have rotted due to soil being too cool and damp. Production begins in 2-3 months from sowing.

Soak plantings regularly and deeply. Furrows between rows will make this job easier; overhead watering may encourage mildew. Mulch plantings to conserve moisture, keep soil temperatures even.

Fertilize with nitrogen only while plants are growing, before beans begin to develop. Too much nitrogen encourages growth at the expense of a crop.

BEETS

Beets are a cool-weather crop, possible only in spring and fall where summers are hot; sow as soon as ground can be worked in spring and for about a month thereafter. In mild-winter climates you can plant them in fall and winter. Maturity is from 55–80 days from seed. An average loam or sandy loam is satisfactory; it must be light enough to "give" as the root expands or roots will be poorly formed. Work in bone meal and a rock potash before planting, along with enough organic matter to lighten soil and hold moisture through the growing season.

Thin seedlings to about 3 inches apart when they are 6 inches tall, and save the thinnings for cooking. Overhead sprinkling for long enough to penetrate root zone will keep both roots and tops crisp. Mulches keep soil temperature and moisture more even.

A light application of organic nitrogen when plants are 5–6 inches high is the only fertilizing beets might need.

BROCCOLI

Broccoli likes the same soil and soil preparation as cabbage. Seedlings planted out will mature in 60–80 days; from seed it may be as much as 150 days to maturity. Although you eat the plant's flower heads, hot weather brings poor quality development.

Water requirements are the same as for cabbage. First harvest will be the flower head on the central stem; pick it when it is hard and green, with about 6 inches of stem. Plants will continue to produce for 2 or 3 months if you keep the lateral heads cut.

Fertilizing: See cabbage, but apply only once or twice before heads form.

BRUSSELS SPROUTS

Brussels sprouts need the same soil and planting considerations as cabbage. Also a cool-season crop, they take about 4 months to mature from seed.

The same watering guidelines as for cabbage apply for Brussels sprouts. The small, cabbage-like heads growing along the central stem are harvested from the bottom upward before they change color. Always leave the top leaves to manufacture food for the plant. If snowy weather arrives and plants are still producing, dig plants, bring them into shelter, put soil around their roots, and continue picking.

Fertilizing: see cabbage.

CABBAGE

Cabbage is the classic cole crop. It is a cool-season plant, so your plantings must be timed so that maturity will be reached before or after hot summer months. Early varieties mature in 90–125 days from seed; late sorts take 125–150 days. In cold-winter areas set out plants as early in spring as possible; plant in mid-summer or early fall (if summers are hot) for late fall and winter crops. From seed it is about 6 weeks until plants can be set out. Prepare soil as described under "Annuals and Vegetables" on page 23, and be generous with the organic matter, phosphorus, and potassium. Cabbage does not like an acid soil. Set plants out in rows that are 30 inches apart, about 18 inches between plants. Plant cabbages firmer and deeper than you would most vegetables since they will form large and topheavy heads.

Maintain an even moisture level; any check in growth from dryness can cause heads to crack. Because they take so long to mature, you can intercrop cabbages with other, faster vegetables such as radishes, lettuce, or spinach.

Every 3–4 weeks fertilize cabbages with a liquid organic nitrogen: blood meal mixed 1 tablespoon to a gallon of water, or liquid fish.

CARROTS

Carrots have requirements similar to those of beets, although they will endure somewhat warmer weather. Roots mature in 65–75 days from sowing. Soil must be sandy to loam free of rocks and lumps which would distort roots; heavy soils produce misshapen, tough carrots. If you have heavy soil, try planting carrots in raised beds that are at least 1 foot above soil surface. Soil preparation is as for beets. Seeds germinate in 2–3 weeks; soil must not dry out during that time. Space rows 12 inches apart.

Thin seedlings to an inch apart, then thin to about 2 inches in a month; by then you will have small, edible carrots. Plantings must be well-drained but can never dry out. Mulch with lightweight material (like straw) to conserve moisture.

Fertilizing is the same as for beets.

CAULIFLOWER

Cauliflower needs the same soil and soil preparation as cabbage but is even more sensitive to heat, frost, and any lack of water. Space plants 2½–3 feet apart in rows 3 feet apart. Maturity is reached in about 2 months from setting out plants. In mild areas, plant in late winter or early spring; otherwise, late summer planting gives a fall harvest.

Because cauliflower is spaced so far apart, takes long to mature, and is very sensitive to a lack of water, intercropping with faster vegetables to shade the soil and to make use of bare space is a good idea. Plant lettuce, radishes, or onion sets when you set out cauliflower; when these are harvested, set out bush beans or peas. Cauliflower will be harvested when the latter crops are mature. When the flower heads start to form, pull the outer leaves over them and fasten with string; this protects from sun and keeps heads white.

Fertilizing: See broccoli.

CELERY

Celery is a cool weather crop. If your summers are hot, set out plants early so they will mature before the warmest weather. Or, plant out seedlings in mid-summer, shade them, and harvest in cool fall weather. It can be a winter crop in mild areas. Start from seed (allow about 10 weeks from sowing to planting out) or set out 3–4-inch plants from a nursery. Soil must be rich in organic matter, well-drained but always moist. Easy way to keep soil cool and blanch (whiten) stems at same time: Dig a trench about 8 inches deep, spade in organic matter, then plant celery seedlings 8–10 inches apart. As they grow, gradually fill in the trench, keeping soil out of the plant's centers.

Water is a prime requirement. Soak soil around plants thoroughly and often (this is easy if you have used the trench method).

Fertilize about every 3 weeks with a liquid organic nitrogen fertilizer. This could be liquid fish, or blood meal mixed 1 tablespoon to a gallon of water.

CHARD

Chard (or Swiss chard) requires no special soil preparation. Follow general directions under "Annuals and Vegetables" on page 23. This vegetable is one of the easiest, for it will continue to produce leaves during hot summer weather when other leaf crops bolt to seed; and, it is hardy enough that in mild areas where winter lows stay above 20°F., it will persist into a second season. Sow seeds in rows and thin to about 6 inches apart; leave 18–24 inches between rows.

A consistent supply of water is the major maintenance requirement; a mulch between rows will help. You can pick chard in 2 ways. When young plants are about a foot high they can be pulled for eating, root and all; for this method, make new plantings about every 4 weeks to have a continuous supply of fresh chard. Or, simply pull off a few outer leaves at a time as you need them and the plant will produce until cut down by winter cold.

Soil prepared with manure, compost, or sludge will probably have enough nutrients to satisfactorily grow chard. However, fertilizing with organic nitrogen during the growing season will produce the finest leaves.

COLLARDS

Collards need the same soil preparation and planting as cabbage; they will endure more heat so can be grown later into the season and farther south. Plant in spring where summers are cool; otherwise plant in mid-summer for fall harvest. Space plants 12-18 inches apart in rows 2 feet apart; if you sow the seeds in place, the thinnings can be used as fine edible greens.

Collards mature in about 75 days. Harvest as you would chard: Pick leaves as you need them.

Fertilizing: See cabbage.

CORN

Maturity is in about 90 days from seed sowing, but corn succeeds best where there is at least a 4-month warm season. For soil preparation, see "Annuals and Vegetables" on page 23. Because it is wind-pollinated, plant corn in several short parallel rows or in hills —never in a single long row. Each plant produces only about 2 ears, so make several sowings 2 weeks apart for a continuous crop. Or, plant early, midseason, and late varieties at one time, then repeat the same varieties about 3 weeks later. Plant seeds 1 inch deep in rows 3 feet apart; thin plants to 12 inches. Space hills 3 feet from center to center; sow 6-7 seeds to each hill, thin to 3 plants.

Water plants deeply, either in furrows between rows or using the hill-and-container method described under cucumbers. Harvest when ear is full and kernels squirt milky juice when punctured. Cook immediately after picking, as sugar changes rapidly to starch and flavor diminishes. Control corn earworm with mineral oil squirted into the silks that project from the end of each ear when the silks turn brown.

Corn appreciates some nitrogen fertilizer during its early growth period only.

CUCUMBERS

Cucumbers grow best in a sandy to loam soil to which has been added a generous amount of organic matter—manure, compost, or sludge, preferably, because of the small amounts of nutrients they will furnish. See general soil preparation directions on page 23 under "Annuals and Vegetables." Cucumbers ripen in 55-70 days from seed; plant them so they will mature in the warmth of summer. Where spring comes late, start them indoors in pots or plant bands, set plants out after frosts pass. Grow them either in rows or on hills. For row planting start them in place 2 feet apart with 4-6 feet between rows; water plants in a furrow between the rows. Row plantings can easily be trained on trellises. For hill planting, place 5 or 6 seeds an inch deep and thin to the 3 strongest, best placed plants; hills should be about 6 feet apart.

(An easy way to water hill plantings is to sink a large container with holes in it in the center of the hill, then plant seeds around the edge; fill the container with water which will soak deeply into plants' root zone.)

Water deeply and mulch plantings with straw, hay, or plastic. Mulch not only conserves moisture but keeps cucumbers dry.

Fertilize with nitrogen only during growth period before blooming.

EGGPLANT

Eggplant requires the same soil preparation as do tomatoes. The differences are that eggplant is slower to start (3-4 weeks to germinate, 10 weeks from sowing until planting out) and needs longer (3 months) to mature. Like peppers, plants are ornamental. Set plants 3 feet apart in rows 3 feet apart. Roots resent disturbance during transplanting; if you start your own, try using peat pots which can be planted without having to remove young plants.

Watering guidelines for peppers apply here, too. About half a dozen eggplants per plant is enough; pinch growth, flower buds to prevent too heavy a fruit set which results in poorer-quality fruit. Harvest when fruits are from $\frac{1}{3}$ to full grown; don't let them hang on plant until the gloss begins to fade and turn dull.

Fertilizing: See tomatoes.

KALE

Kale is planted as you would cabbage. It matures in 60-80 days; plant in mid-summer for fall and winter crops, in fall or late winter for late winter and early spring crops in mild climates.

Cut leaves gradually (like chard) for cooking; harvest entire plant (and use inner leaves) for raw greens.

Fertilizing: See cabbage.

KOHLRABI

Kohlrabi thrives only in cool seasons and cool climates. Prepare soil the same as for cabbage but go heavy on the organic matter— plants need constant moisture for good roots. Sow in rows 18 inches apart beginning 2 weeks after average date of last frost; thin plants to 4 inches apart in the rows. Plant again in late fall in mild-winter climates. Kohlrabi matures in 55-60 days. Harvest roots when they are about the size of an egg.

Fertilizing: See cabbage.

LEEKS

Leeks need the same soil and preparation as onions; they will mature in about 100 days. Start in flats from seed, transplant seedlings to the ground, about 4 inches apart, when they are 4 inches high. The shank of a leek plant is usually blanched, either by mounding soil up around it or by covering it with a paper collar. A simpler way to accomplish this is to plant seedlings in a trench that is 3-4 inches deep; as the plant grows, gradually fill in the trench with soil.

The chief maintenance requirement is a steady water supply. Trenched plantings will generally dry out more slowly, require water less often than plantings at soil grade level.

No fertilizing should be necessary.

LETTUCE

Lettuce does not require a rich soil. Directions under "Annuals and Vegetables" on page 23 will be satisfactory. Plants mature very rapidly so that you can sow seeds every week to 2 weeks to keep a new crop coming along; it's easiest to sow in place in rows 12–18 inches apart and thin seedlings to about 6 inches.

Water lettuce regularly and generously. Use a mulch or grow plants close together and thin plantings gradually so leaves always cover soil. Leaf lettuce may be picked a leaf at a time like chard or harvested all at once. Head lettuce must be picked entire; otherwise quality deteriorates. Lettuce is very sensitive to hot weather and will bolt to seed at the expense of leaf production. For summer lettuce in warm climates plant it where it will be shaded during hottest part of the day—such as in the afternoon shade of a taller crop. Birds relish young lettuce plants; cover with chicken wire or netting if this is a problem.

Because lettuce matures so quickly, the nutrients should be in the soil at planting time. Phosphorus and potash, worked into the soil in early spring, should last out the season. Nitrogen could be added again in mid-season.

MELONS

Melons require the same soil preparation and culture as do cucumbers, but they are too heavy to be trellised. Melons are often grown in gently-rounded raised beds—6 feet from center to center except for watermelons which need an 8 foot distance. On the south slope of this rounded bed, make a furrow about 10 inches wide and 6 inches deep; run water into furrows until they are filled. Then, every 3 feet along the furrow (except for watermelons: every 8 feet) scrape away about an inch of soil in an 8-10-inch circle about 6 inches above the furrow (be sure this area has been thoroughly moistened by the previous irrigation). Scatter 6 or 7 seeds in the circle, place ½ inch of moist soil over them and press it down; add the remaining ½ inch of soil but don't firm it down. Mulch lightly to conserve moisture. Barring unusually hot weather, no watering should be necessary until the seed has germinated. As soon as plants are established, thin out to 2 for each circle; train them north, over the top of the mound.

Water and mulch melons as you would cucumbers.

Fertilizing: See cucumbers.

MUSTARD

Mustard is not particular as to soil; see general directions under "Annuals and Vegetables" on page 23. Sow in place at 3 week intervals and thin to 6 inches apart for a continuous supply. Plants mature in 35–60 days and can be grown all year in mild climates.

Regular watering is all mustard asks. Harvest leaves as they approach maturity (before leaf edges turn red-brown).

If soil has been prepared with generous amount of organic matter no fertilizing should be necessary.

ONIONS

A sandy to loam soil is best. Add generous amounts of organic matter, rock potash, and bone meal before planting. Onions are grown from sets (tiny onion bulbs), seedlings, or seed. Plant either from winter through April in mild winter climates, or in early spring where winters are cold. Onions from seed are slow to mature (4 months) but the thinnings will provide plenty of green onions; from sets or from seedlings you may have dry onions in 95 days. Sow seeds in rows 15-18 inches apart, thin to 3 inches apart. If you plant sets or seedlings, space them 3 inches apart.

Steady water is the main maintenance requirement. When green tops begin to yellow, bend them over to the ground; all growing energy will be diverted to the bulb.

No additional fertilizer is needed.

PEAS

Peas, in contrast to beans, are a cool-season plant. Where summers are hot, sow as soon as ground is workable; it takes 60-80 days from seed to maturity. Sow varieties that mature at different times for a longer harvest season. In cool-summer areas make successive plantings. For general soil preparation see "Annuals and Vegetables" on page 23. Peas prefer loam soils with much organic matter added. They must have good drainage and a non-acid soil. Water the planting area thoroughly *before* planting, then not again until plants break through surface.

Irrigate in furrows between the rows; mulch to conserve moisture. Regularly pick all pea pods—peas are seeds and if left on the plant will cause the plant to stop production. Watch for aphids and control them as described on page 50.

Fertilizing: See beans.

PEPPERS

Peppers make very attractive ornamental plants. Prepare the soil as you would for tomatoes and observe the same timing in planting out. Space peppers 18 inches apart in rows 2 feet apart; they will mature in 65-85 days from planting.

Pepper plants must never be constantly saturated, but an even moisture supply is necessary for good production. Water in furrows between rows, or in basins around individual plants. Peppers that are to be used fresh should be picked while firm and crisp. Hot peppers for drying should ripen (and change color) on the plant.

Fertilizing: See tomatoes.

POTATOES

Potatoes take much space for the amount they yield. Figure an average of 6 potatoes per plant. Prepare the soil in fall for planting the following spring, adding generous amounts of manure or other organic materials plus phosphorus and potash. Spade all in thoroughly and let soil lie fallow until planting. Potatoes prefer a light to loamy soil free of rocks or lumps for well-shaped tubers. They are a cool-season plant so should be set out in early spring or as soon as soil can be worked. Dig a trench 4–6 inches deep and place potato pieces (with 2 eyes, each) cut side down and 18 inches apart; fill trench to 2 inches from the top. Add remaining soil up to ground level when the young plants reach about 1 foot tall.

Potatoes need continuous moisture but not a saturated soil. A mulch will help keep moisture even and will foil the potato tuber moth which lays eggs for its destructive larvae in cracks in the ground. Dig early, or "new," potatoes when the plants flower. Otherwise, dig tubers after tops die (they will also store in the ground).

Fertilizing is the same as for beets.

RADISHES

Radishes are nearly foolproof if planted in the right seasons. They are a cool-weather crop but mature in only 3 weeks to a month. They prefer a light to loamy soil but require no special preparations (see "Annuals and Vegetables" on page 23). Sow in early spring until arrival of warm weather; then plant again when cooler fall temperatures arrive. In mild-winter areas they can be grown through those months. Sow in rows a foot apart and thin plants to a 1-inch spacing. Because radishes are so quick to mature you can easily interplant them with almost any of the slower vegetables. Harvest them promptly at maturity, otherwise they become tough and pithy.

You can give radishes a fertilizing of liquid fish or of blood meal dissolved 1 tablespoon to a gallon of water, but this may be unnecessary in a reasonably fertile soil.

RHUBARB

Several varieties are available, with red or green leaf-stalks; all are very ornamental plants. Rhubarb prefers a loam to clay loam to which quantities of organic matter have been added; drainage must be good. Growth is best where winters are cold enough to freeze the soil for a few inches and where summers are moist but cool. Depending upon climate, any time from fall through spring is the planting season; mulch plants well if you fall-plant where winters are cold. Because rhubarb remains in place for a number of years, be sure to mix a generous sprinkling of bone meal and rock potash into the root zone soil. Plant with the top of each division at the soil line, spacing them about 3 feet apart. If your summers are hot and dry, make sure plants will get mid-day shade then.

Rhubarb needs plenty of water (but not waterlogged soil) during its growing seasons. A mulch will help keep soil temperatures even. Like asparagus, rhubarb should not be picked during its first year and only lightly harvested during the second. In the third year you can pick leaf-stalks for 4–5 weeks; older plants can be harvested for up to 2 months. Pull, don't cut, the leaf-stalks from the base of the plants, and never remove all leaves from a single plant. Stop harvesting whenever slender leaf-stalks appear. Cut out any flowering stems that appear. Note: rhubarb leaves are poisonous.

Give plants a liberal fertilization with organic nitrogen in early spring and again during mid-summer especially when picking has been heavy. Mulches of manure, compost, or sludge will also furnish some additional nutrients.

SPINACH

Spinach prefers a light, thoroughly dug soil with abundant organic matter added but will not grow well where soil is acid. It must have a cool, moist growing season. In hot summer areas, sow seeds early so that plants can take advantage of as much cooler spring weather as you have; plants mature in 45–50 days. Sow successive crops at about 2-week intervals until weather becomes too warm (you can sow the later crops where they will receive midday shade). Begin again in mid- to late summer for fall spinach crops. In mild areas, sow in fall for winter harvest.

Spinach revels in plenty of water and actually prefers overhead sprinkling. A mulch will help hold moisture. Pick leaves as you need them or harvest entire plants.

You should apply a rapidly-available nitrogen fertilizer while the crop is actively growing. Try liquid fish, or blood meal dissolved 1 tablespoon in a gallon of water.

SQUASH AND PUMPKINS

Squash and Pumpkins need the same soil and preparation as cucumbers. Summer squash matures in 60-65 days, winter squash and pumpkins need about 120 days. Plant bush types (summer squash) 2 feet apart in rows 4-5 feet apart, or in hills spaced about 4-5 feet apart (see cucumbers). Winter types and pumpkins grow on running vines; plant in rows that are 5 feet apart or on hills spaced 8 feet apart each way. See cucumbers for hill planting, melons for row planting in slightly raised beds.

Watering is important but should not cover crowns of plants or keep soil constantly moist in that area.

Water in hill-wells (see cucumbers) or in furrows between rows. Mulch to conserve soil moisture and to keep fruit dry. Pick summer squash before it is fully grown (you should be able to pierce skin with your fingernail); harvest pumpkins before hard frosts arrive; winter squash should mature on vine before picking.

Fertilizing: See cucumbers.

TOMATOES

Tomatoes mature in 2-3 months from setting out plants. To perform their best they must have warm days and nights; plants will grow well in cooler weather, but fruit is less and poorer in quality. For soil preparation, see "Annuals and Vegetables" on page 23; tomatoes are very deep rooted, so dig the soil deeper than usual for most other vegetables. If set out too early, plants sit there until soil warms up. Sow seeds indoors 6-8 weeks before average date of latest frost. Plants root along the stems, so set them out with about 1/2 the stem covered by soil. Space plants 12-18 inches apart if they are to be staked, 2-4 feet apart if they will spread along the ground. Staking is good in cooler climates as fruit will be exposed more to the sun. In warmer climates, fruit on plants running on the ground will be beneficially shaded by the leaves.

Because they are so deep rooted, tomatoes require less frequent watering, but still appreciate a mulch to maintain a relatively even soil moisture level. For staked plants, tie up main stem and keep side stems pinched out as they appear; when the main stem reaches the top of the stake, pinch out the tip. In cool, damp climates, mildew may be a problem. If tomato hornworms appear, pick them by hand. Too much nitrogen produces much growth but little fruit. Nutrients incorporated at planting time (and nitrogen in manure, sludge, or compost) should be sufficient.

TURNIPS AND RUTABAGAS

Turnips and rutabagas need the same soil preparation as do beets. Both are cool-season crops; turnips mature in about 2 months, rutabagas in 3. In cold-winter and in hot-summer climates, sow them in early spring and again in mid- or late-summer. Space rows about 16 inches apart; thin turnips to 2–3 inches, rutabagas to 3–4 inches.

Steady moisture is necessary; use a mulch if you can. Pull turnips for greens (or for turnips and greens) when roots are about 3/4 mature—the size of a large egg. Rutabagas will keep in the ground but turnips become woody. Nor do turnips store well: They emit a foul odor.

Fertilize as you would beets.

How to Grow Fruits and Berries

APPLES

Apples are among the most cold-tolerant of fruit trees, but climate adaptability varies according to variety (especially true for adaptability to *mild* winters). Best growth and fruit production is in deep, well-drained soils, but trees will tolerate some heavy, poorly-drained ones. Some varieties need a pollenizer to set fruit. Plant 1- or 2-year-old trees in fall; cut back to 2½ feet. See "Bare-root planting," page 26, for planting directions. Mature trees may reach 20 feet tall with a 40 foot spread, so space accordingly. Many varieties are available on dwarfing or semi-dwarfing rootstocks which will grow into 8 to 15 foot trees.

Dwarf trees are shallow-rooted, must be staked permanently at planting time to prevent mature tree from tipping over. Keep bud union of dwarf trees several inches above soil level; if planted too low, the graft may grow its own roots and lose the dwarf character.

The first spring (after you have cut the new tree back at planting), select 3-4 strong branches and a leader; remove any other branches. Thereafter, prune only to shape the tree. In snowy areas and rural locations, protect trunks of young trees by enclosing them in a wire cylinder inserted 1-2 inches into the ground; this will foil rodents, deer which can eat the bark, often girdling and killing the tree. Spray apple trees with oil spray in the late winter.

Fruit quality goes down if trees have too much nitrogen. Give established trees about ¼ pound actual nitrogen each year in early spring before bloom is out.

APRICOTS

Apricots flower very early in spring; consequently, fruit production is chancy in regions subject to late frosts which follow warmer weather. To grow apricots in these areas, plant trees in a northern exposure (but not in shade) which will warm up the slowest; varieties grafted on myrobalan plum can be planted in fairly heavy clay soils (as long as water will drain away), and because clays warm up last of the soil types the trees will start growth later in the season. In milder climates, select varieties with low winter chilling requirement. Plant in late winter (mild climates) or early spring; see "Peaches and Nectarines" for directions.

Cut back newly-planted tree to about 2½ feet and select 3 branches to form a balanced scaffold. The following winter, select the strongest branch to be the leader, then shorten all 3 branches to no less than 2 feet but maintaining the definite superiority of the leader. Otherwise, pruning is needed only to maintain good structure.

Fertilize apricots with no more nitrogen than is recommended for peaches.

BLACKBERRIES

Blackberries are of 2 basic kinds: the trailing varieties grown on the West Coast, and the more hardy, stiff-caned, upright kinds grown in the Midwest and East. All blackberries require a deep soil and full sun. Follow the general directions under "Perennials, Bulbs, and Bulb-like plants" on page 25. Easiest to handle if grown in rows, the trailing kinds trained on horizontal wires. Plant 3 inches deep and about 4 feet apart, in early spring.

Blackberries have perennial roots but canes are biennial: New canes emerge and grow one year, produce fruiting side branches the second year, then die back. Where grown on a wire trellis, train only the 1-year-old canes on the trellis. After fruit harvest, cut all fruited canes to the ground. Then train canes of the current season on the trellis and prune to 6-8 feet; thin them out to all but 12 to 16 canes. These will produce side branches during remainder of growing season; cut these side branches back to 12 inches in early spring. With the new spring growth, small branches that will bear fruit will grow from the side branches. Thin out semi-upright varieties to 4 to 8 canes and spread fan-wise on the trellis. Upright varieties need no trellis but are easier to handle tied to a wire about 2½ feet above ground; select about 4 canes, cut back to 3 feet, and tie where they cross the wire.

Mulch plantings generously every year; manure and compost are good choices as they will supply small amounts of nutrients. Spray in winter and again as buds are about to break with lime-sulfur.

A light fertilization with organic nitrogen at blossom time should be sufficient if manure, compost, or sludge is used liberally as a mulch. Too much nitrogen only creates rank cane growth but no significant increase in berry yield.

BLUEBERRIES

Blueberries need cool, moist, acid soil that drains well. A sandy to light loam is best, well-fortified with plenty of peat moss or other acidic organic matter. Plants are highly ornamental, with attractive small flowers, fruit, and good fall color. Plant 3 feet apart as an informal hedge; in larger plantings, as shrubs, space 4-5 feet apart. Most varieties are upright to 6 feet or more; a few are rather sprawling and under 5 feet. Plant 2 different varieties to assure pollination. Blueberries have shallow roots which must not dry out; keep plants well watered, and mulch with from 4-6 inches of sawdust, ground bark, or other wood products. Prune to prevent overbearing (which decreases fruit quality). Keep first-year plants from bearing by stripping off flowers. On older plants cut back ends of twigs to a point where fruit buds are widely spaced; or, simply remove some of the oldest branches each year. Remove all weak shoots. Spreading varieties seldom make multiple stems from ground level, so pruning will consist of thinning wood, tipping new branches.

Fertilize lightly in spring with cottonseed meal if your soil is not strongly acid; it will contribute to the acidity blueberries must have. If you mulch with raw sawdust (or other wood products) be sure to add enough extra nitrogen to compensate for that amount the sawdust will use in its decomposition (see chart on pages 12-13).

CHERRIES

Cherries are at their best in a deep, well-drained soil; on shallow or poorly-drained soils they will decline and die. All cherries — sweet and sour — have a high chilling requirement (need many winter hours below 45°) and therefore are not adapted to mild-winter areas. Because they bloom early they are subject to frost damage; best planting sites are the same as those recommended for peaches in cold-winter areas: on hillsides, and near large bodies of water. Fall planting is best, as cherry roots are sensitive to drying out after plants are dug; spring-planted trees are likely to have been out of the ground for several months. Space sweet cherries about 30 feet apart; they may not always occupy that much space but fruit needs sunlight to ripen. Sour cherries may be planted as close as 20 feet. Planting is the same as for peaches. Two trees are needed to produce fruit on sweet cherries, and you must choose the second tree carefully. No combination of these will produce fruit: 'Bing', 'Lambert', 'Royal Ann'. These varieties will pollenize any other cherry: 'Black Tartarian', 'Corum', 'Deacon', 'Republican', 'Sam', and 'Van'.

Young trees, at least, should be mulched. Pruning during the first several years should maintain a definite leader with development of strong, subordinate scaffold branches. When mature size is reached, only prune to shape, eliminate weak wood, and to thin top and sides so that sunlight will reach all parts of the tree to permit even fruit distribution. Birds are notorious cherry predators; you can either cover an entire tree with netting or plant mulberries nearby as decoy fruit. Cherries must be ripened on the tree.

Fertilize as you would peaches and nectarines.

CURRANTS AND GOOSEBERRIES

Currants and Gooseberries require substantially the same culture. Before planting, make sure it is legal to grow these fruits in your region; in some areas it is prohibited because they are alternate hosts to white pine blister rust. Both are very cold-tolerant and prefer the cooler climates of the Northeast and Northwest. In contrast to most fruits, they prefer a loam to heavy soil, moist but still well-drained. In warmer areas of the South, Midwest, and West, they will do best (although not their *very* best) if shaded by trees or buildings. Plant in fall, about 5 feet apart each way. Prepare soil as outlined under "Perennials, Bulbs, and Bulblike Plants" on page 25. Despite their preference for heavy soils they like organic matter mixed into the soil at planting time.

Currants and gooseberries are shallow-rooted and so should be thoroughly mulched to keep root zone cool and moist. They bear at the base of year-old wood and on spurs on 2- and 3-year wood. Prune so that you keep a balance of 1-, 2-, and 3-year canes; prune out older canes and weak growth.

In early spring, give plantings a very light application of organic nitrogen. A generous mulch of manure or compost may be sufficient to supply their nutrient needs.

GRAPES

To get quality fruit you must choose a variety that fits your climate. The 2 basic classes are: European—high heat requirements, cold tolerance to about 5°; and American—moderate heat requirements, cold tolerance well below 0°. Hybrids between classes are available. If your climate is cooler, or growing season shorter, than ideal: Look for early-ripening varieties or create a warmer climate by giving the vine the added heat of a south-facing wall. Vines are deep-rooted, grow best in deep soils; drainage *must* be good, hence they prefer loam or sandy loam. Plant year-old plants in fall or early spring; set them deeply, leaving only the top bud exposed (mound soil over bud in cold-winter areas when planting in fall).

During the growing season, water

. . . Grapes (continued)

to a depth of at least 3 feet to develop a good root system on young vines. Mildew is a serious pest of European varieties (most American varieties are immune). To control, dust the vines with sulfur when shoots are 6 inches long, again when they are 12-15 inches, then every 2 weeks until harvest. Pruning depends upon what class the variety you grow belongs to, and whether you are growing it for fruit production or for purely ornamental use. Most European grapes are spur-pruned; Americans are cane-pruned. For spur pruning, let the vine sprawl and develop as many leaves as possible during the first year to manufacture food for developing roots. The first winter, prune out all but one sturdy cane; shorten it to the 3 lowest buds and let these grow to 12 inches in spring—then select the strongest shoot and train it upright to form the permanent trunk (remove the

other 2 shoots); when this shoot reaches a foot above the point on an arbor, trellis, or fence where you want it to branch out, cut it back to the fence and let 2 strong shoots develop on either side of the stem (any side shoots that develop on these 2 "arms" should be pinched back to 10 inches). That winter—the second one after planting—cut the shoots back to the 2 arms. During spring and summer, more shoots will grow from the 2 arms; when winter comes, thin these out so that shoots will be spaced 6 to 10 inches apart, then cut these remaining shoots back to 2 buds. Each bud will give 2 fruiting canes the next summer; in the following winter, cut out one entirely, shorten the other to 2 buds. Pruning in subsequent years follows the same pattern: a cut back to 2 buds on previous year's growth will produce 2 fruiting canes; always cut out one of these and prune the other back to 2 buds. Cane pruning for American varieties is the same as spur pruning in the first 2 years

except that in the second summer you pinch out the stem tip a foot above the desired fence, arbor, or trellis height. Let side shoots grow on upper third of the plant, cut off shoots on bottom two-thirds; tie the vine near the top and at middle. That winter, cut off the main stem right through the bud just above the fence top or wire. Remove side branches below midpoint; of the remaining branches remove all but 2 to 4 and cut them back to 2-bud spurs. The winter after that, you will have 2 canes that developed from each one you cut the previous winter. For each of these 2, cut one as a fruiting cane (leave 8 to 12 buds) and cut the other back to a 2-bud spur. In subsequent winters, cut off old fruiting cane from previous year's growth; then, leave one cane that grew from last year's 2-bud spur to be a fruiting cane and cut the other back to a 2-bud spur.

Before growth starts in spring, give established vines 2-3 ounces actual nitrogen.

PEACHES AND NECTARINES

Peaches and Nectarines differ by variety in their tolerance of cold or of mild winters. First consideration is to select varieties which are adapted to your climate; generally, they are a risk where winter temperatures go below −15°, but planting on a hillside where coldest air drains past to low-lying areas) or near large bodies of water (which moderate winter lows) may let you grow these fruits in areas otherwise too cold for them. Warm-winter regions can select from varieties which need less than the usual chilling requirement. Plant in fall wherever possible, no less than 20 feet apart; cold-winter

areas will have to plant in early spring. Of all stone fruits these prefer the lightest soils: sand to loam; good drainage is essential. Dig planting hole large enough to accommodate roots without bending; add generous amounts of phosphorus and potassium to root zone (see "Bare-root planting," page 26). Cut back the main stem to about 30 inches and shorten any remaining lateral branches to an inch; new branches will form below the cut.

Young trees, at least, should be mulched. After first year's growth, select 3 well-placed branches (at different heights and pointing in different directions) for scaffold limbs; remove all other branches.

On mature trees, each dormant season, cut off $2/3$ of the previous year's growth by removing 2 of every 3 branches formed last year; or head back each branch to $1/3$ its length. Or, head back some branches and cut out others entirely. Spray in late fall and again in early spring with lime-sulfur or Bordeaux mixture to control peach leaf curl. Sprays containing lime-sulfur and oil will control both leaf curl and scale.

Young trees will appreciate 1-2 ounces actual nitrogen applied in early spring. As trees grow, increase the amount until mature trees get about 1 pound actual nitrogen. One to $1\frac{1}{2}$ feet of new growth per year is normal.

PEARS

Pears will accept poor drainage and neglect better than other fruit trees. Ideally, they should have the same soil and planting as apples, but spaced about 20 feet apart each way. For planting instructions see "Bare-root planting," page 26. Dwarf pears are also sold. Prune

newly-planted pears as you would apples and treat them similarly thereafter.

The major enemy of pears is fireblight, the remedy for which is to cut out and destroy the blackened, diseased wood. It attacks primarily young, vigorous wood. Therefore, prune trees only to shape them,

limiting cuts to smaller branches if possible, as heavy pruning may stimulate vigorous, susceptible growth.

Too much nitrogen gives over-vigorous growth which is subject to fireblight. Use no nitrogen fertilizer unless trees show obvious signs of a deficiency (see pages 14-16).

PLUM AND PRUNE

Plum and Prune varieties most often planted are derived from either a European or a Japanese species; hybrids between Japanese and American species have been developed which adapt to the midwestern states. Both Japanese and European varieties grow 15-20 feet high and about as wide. European varieties bloom late and are better adapted to areas with late frosts or cool, rainy spring weather than are the early-blooming Japanese sorts. Many varieties need another variety growing nearby as a pollenizer in order to set fruit.

Planting directions (and location of plantings) are the same as for peaches and nectarines, but plums will tolerate—and appreciate—heavier soils.

After planting a plum, select 4 or 5 strong branches that grow in different directions and that are spaced at least 6 inches from one another on the trunk to be the main structure; remove all other branches, then cut back framework branches to lateral branches. Train young trees to a vase shape. If tree tends to grow upright, cut to outside branches; if it is spreading, cut to inside branches. European plums do not branch as freely as Japanese kinds, so selection of framework branches may be more limited. Japanese plums often make tremendous annual shoot growth, necessitating rather heavy pruning. European varieties are more restrained, usually require just thinning out of annual shoot growth; prune to avoid formation of V-shaped crotches. Japanese prunes tend to bear too heavily and require more fruit thinning (spaced from 4-6 inches apart) than European sorts.

Orchardists give Japanese plums 1-3 pounds of actual nitrogen a year, 1-2 pounds for European varieties.

RASPBERRIES

Raspberries fall into 2 groups the red and the black—which require somewhat different pruning and maintenance. All raspberries, however, must have a definitely well-drained soil. Otherwise, follow the general directions under "Perennials, Bulbs, and Bulb-like Plants" on page 25. Plant all kinds 2½-3 feet apart in rows 7-9 feet apart, setting roots about an inch deeper than they grew originally. Cut back the cane that rises from the roots, leaving only enough stub to serve as a marker. The plant should produce 3-5 sturdy canes the first year.

Red raspberries can become a wild thicket unless controlled. Each year cut out canes that have fruited and select 8-12 strong canes of the current season's growth that come up near the crown; remove all others, especially those that come up at a distance from the crown. In spring before growth begins, cut back to 4½-5½ feet; these are easiest to handle if supported between 2 horizontal wires or stakes. Fall-bearing raspberries ripen canes earlier in summer and fruit near the top of the cane; cut off the upper portion that has borne fruit—then the lower parts will fruit next spring. Cut out the cane after it has fruited along its entire length.

For black raspberries, pinch out tips of new canes when they reach 18–24 inches; this forces branches to grow which are cut back to about 12 inches the next spring and will then bear fruit. Plenty of water during the growing season is essential. Mulch plantings generously every year; manure and compost are good choices as they will supply small amounts of nutrients. Don't plant black raspberries where solanaceous vegetables (tomatoes, peppers, eggplant, or potatoes) have been grown recently as they can carry a wilt disease that affects the berries.

Fertilizing: See blackberries.

STRAWBERRIES

See "Perennials, Bulbs, and Bulb-like Plants," page 25, for general soil preparation directions. Strawberries are not particular to soil as long as it is well-drained, well-supplied with organic matter, and sunny. Plant in early spring; mild-winter areas can plant in late summer or fall and get berries the next spring. To harvest a big crop of berries, plant in rows. If soil is heavy or poorly drained, set plants in rows along raised mounds 5-6 inches high and 28 inches from center to center. Use the furrows between mounds for irrigation and feeding. Set plants 14-16 inches apart. If soil drains well or if furrow irrigation would be difficult, plant on flat ground 14-18 inches apart in rows 18 inches apart, and water by overhead sprinkling. It is best to use a flat bed wherever salinity is a problem. Another method: Set plants 2-3 feet apart in rows 4-5 feet apart, let runners fill in until plants are 7-10 inches apart, then keep additional runners pinched off; keep rows 20-30 inches wide. If you need just a few berries, plant a dozen or so plants, spaced 14-18 inches apart in a sunny patch within a flower or vegetable garden, or even in boxes or tubs. Set plants carefully; crown should be just above soil level, topmost roots ¼ inch beneath soil level (buried crowns rot; exposed roots dry out).

Mulch plantings to conserve moisture, keep weeds down, and keep berries clean. Especially in the bearing season, strawberries need frequent deep soaking. Pick off blooms the first year on newly-set plants (or until mid-summer on everbearing varieties) to allow plants to develop. In cold-winter regions, mulch in late fall with straw or pine needles to a depth of 3-4 inches.

Lightly fertilize with nitrogen twice each year—once when growth begins, again after the first crop.

How to Grow Herbs

Since ancient times, man has cultivated or gathered certain plants for their fragrance, flavor, or healing qualities. These plants are what we collectively call "herbs". Even today, they are grown for their fragrances and for use in cooking—and in addition, many are versatile, durable garden ornamentals. Some creep along the ground; others are shrublike and can be clipped to make formal hedges or grown informally in shrub or perennial borders. Many make attractive container plants. Listed here are some favorite herbs. Before using fresh herbs, wash the leaves with water—especially if toxic sprays have been used in the area.

Basil. Also called sweet basil, this annual has leaves in varying shades of green and purple; variety 'Dark Opal' has larger, dark bronze-purple foliage. Plants grow to 2 feet. Basil needs full sun and warm soil. Sow seeds in early spring and set out plants after frost, spaced 10-12 inches apart. Water them regularly. Use fresh or dried leaves in salads, sauces, vegetable dishes.

Chives. Perennial, grasslike clumps grow 2 feet tall under favorable conditions. Chives like moist soil well-supplied with organic matter; grow them in sun in all but the hottest climates. You can start plants from seed but it is easier to divide older clumps. Chives are evergreen in mild climates; where winters are severe they go dormant, but you can pot small divisions and grow them indoors through the winter. Use cut leaves for a mild onion flavor in salads, soups, and with cheeses.

Dill. This is a 3-4-foot annual with feathery leaves and flowers in wide, flat-topped clusters. Sow seeds in full sun, average soil, where you want the plants (seedlings don't transplant easily), and thin to 18 inches apart. Sow seeds several times in spring and summer for a constant supply. Seeds or leaves impart the dill flavor to pickles, while fresh or dried leaves are used in salads, meat dishes (especially lamb), and sauces.

Garlic. You can grow this onion relative from seed, but the usual method is to plant small bulbs (called "cloves"). In mild-winter areas, plant in fall for early summer harvest; where winters are cold, plant in early spring. Set the cloves base downward, 1-2 inches deep and 2-3 inches apart. Harvest when leafy tops fall over; air-dry the bulbs, remove tops and roots, and store them in a cool place. Small amounts of minced garlic cloves can be used to season salads, sauces, and meats.

Lavender. Several species are grown for the aroma of leaves and flowers; plant heights range from 8 inches to 4 feet. All need full sun and a loose, fast-draining soil. Give them occasional water if summers are rainless—otherwise, they need none. The characteristic lavender fragrance comes from the flowers. Cut the flower clusters (or strip flowers from their stems) just as first blooms open; then dry them in a cool, shady place.

Marjoram. This is a perennial in mild climates; where winters are freezing, carry it through winter as a house plant. Leaves are tiny, oval, gray-green on a 1-2-foot plant. Grow plants from seed, cuttings, or root divisions—in full sun and fairly moist soil. They become woody unless flowers and older growth are trimmed off. Use fresh or dried leaves as seasoning for salads, vinegars, meats, and sauces.

Mint. All mint species are perennials that grow from creeping underground stems which can become invasive. Best growth is in light, moist soil in part shade. Use fresh leaves as a garnish or in cold drinks, fresh or dried leaves in cooking—especially with lamb.

Oregano. Like marjoram (a close relative), this is an annual in cold-winter areas unless wintered indoors. Plants reach about 2½ feet, with medium-sized oval leaves and purplish-pink flowers. You can grow it from divisions as well as from seed, since plants spread by underground runners. Give oregano full sun and good drainage, moderate watering, in a soil with some organic materials added. Fresh or dried leaves are used in many dishes and sauces, especially Spanish and Italian ones.

Parsley. Plants grow 6-12 inches tall with tufted dark green leaves. Parsley is a biennial but is most satisfactorily grown from new sowing every year. Plants tolerate various growing conditions but perform best in full sun and good, fairly moist soil. To aid the normally-slow seed germination, soak seeds in warm water for 24 hours before planting; even then, they may not sprout for several weeks. Sow seeds in place and thin young plants to 6-8 inches apart. Use fresh leaves as a garnish, either fresh or dried in salads and vegetable dishes.

Rosemary. There are several forms of rosemary—from a shrubby ground cover to upright, 6-foot bushes. The almost needlelike leaves are gray-green to rich green, and early spring flowers vary, by variety, from light blue to bright blue-violet. Plants endure hot sun and poor soil, and will need little or no water (once established) except in desert areas. Prime requisite is good drainage. Start plants from cuttings or layers; established plants often form roots wherever a branch touches soil. Where winters are freezing, grow plants in containers and shift them indoors when weather becomes too cold. Fresh or dried leaves are used to flavor meats and casserole dishes.

Sage. This is a 2-foot, shrubby perennial with narrow gray-green leaves. It will flourish in good or poor soil as long as drainage is good. Individual plants are good for only 4-5 years, so start new ones from seeds, cuttings, or layers in time to replace ageing ones. Sage also grows well in containers—bring it indoors for a supply of winter herbs. The dried leaves are used to season poultry and stuffings for meats.

Thyme. There are ground cover types and shrubby forms, but all thymes are perennials grown from seed, cuttings, or layers. Give them well-drained and fairly dry soil in full sun. Plants also grow well in containers. The fresh or dried leaves are used in preparing meats, fish, poultry, vegetables, and sauces.

How to Grow Ornamental Plants

DECIDUOUS SHRUBS AND TREES

These plants characterize the landscapes of the Northeast, Midwest, and mountain states—the definitely cold-winter regions. Tolerance to low temperatures varies among the different plants in the deciduous category; if you want to try growing a plant slightly tender for your general climate, see the advice under "Broad-leafed evergreen plants" for how to select the warmest spots in your garden. Many of these plants are sold in fall, winter, and early spring as bare-root plants; for general instructions on how to plant these, see "Bare-root planting" on page 26. It is important to keep the roots of all plants—but especially of bare-root specimens—moist before planting. If roots appear to be at all dry, soak the root system in water for several hours prior to planting.

Many flowering deciduous shrubs fall into one of two categories: those which flower on wood produced in the current season, and those which flower on wood produced the previous year. The first group is pruned in late winter or early spring so as to produce a quantity of new growth that will bear flowers; the exact methods will vary somewhat, depending upon the particular plant's growth habit. The second group—those that flower on year-old wood—should be pruned immediately after flowering so that new wood will be produced throughout the rest of the year for flowering the next year; again, exact methods vary according to the plant involved. A number of deciduous flowering shrubs require no pruning except what is necessary to shape the plant. This advice also applies generally to deciduous trees. For watering and winter-protection, see "Broad-leafed evergreen plants."

Most deciduous plants have a definite seasonal growth cycle; fertilizing instructions are the same as for broad-leafed evergreen plants, but with deciduous kinds it is often more easy to predict the timing.

Roses

Most often you see roses planted in beds by themselves. Although it represents considerable labor, the best planting preparation is to double-dig the area the rose bed will occupy (see page 23). If this is not practical, at least prepare the planting hole soil to twice a spade's depth and plant according to instructions on page 26 for "Bare root planting." In mild climates, set the plant in its hole so that the bud union—where top growth emerges from the short shank above the roots—is just above the soil level; where winter temperatures consistently drop below 10°, set union just below soil level. Winter is the best planting season in mild climates; the North and other cold-winter areas plant in spring; either fall or spring planting may be done where winters are only moderately cold. Mound moist soil around the canes of a newly planted bush and remove it only when new growth begins. Selection of varieties is important: Some are more cold-hardy than others; some prefer cool, moist weather while others revel in that which is hot and dry; resistance to mildew, to rust, and to black spot also varies.

Water is a prime requisite for actively-growing roses, and—given good drainage—they will thrive on frequent deep soakings. A mulch will help keep moisture level even, but wait until soil has warmed up in spring before applying one. Methods of pruning depend upon the type of rose, your climate, and even the individual variety's growth habit. However, in pruning any rose the objective is a symmetrical plant with a well-balanced arrangement of canes, a center open to light and air, and its flowering branches growing outward and upward. Best time to prune is at the end of the dormant season when the large, plump buds begin to swell. Always remove all dead and weak wood. Where winter temperatures reliably fall below 10°, most hybrid teas, floribundas, and grandifloras will need winter protection. Often a mound of soil 8-12 inches high over the base of a plant is sufficient; in areas that experience −20° or more, you may need to provide additional protective insulation of evergreen boughs or straw over the mounds. Winter climates vary so greatly that it is a wise practice to get local advice on protection requirements for your particular area. The American Rose Society, 4048 Roselea Place, Columbus, Ohio, 43014, will give you the name of their Consulting Rosarian in your area; if none exists in your area, consult your county agricultural extension service.

Apply no fertilizer to the soil surface the first year. Thereafter, the first fertilizing in spring comes as growth reaches an inch or two in length. Subsequent applications should be timed in relation to bloom period; apply fertilizer when a blooming period has come to an end and new growth is just beginning for the next period. In cold-winter regions, the last fertilization for the season should not be later than the end of August; otherwise the bushes may produce new growth so late that it will be severely damaged by freezing weather. The first application in spring should be of bone meal (from a handful to a cupful,—depending on the plant's size) and an organic nitrogen fertilizer—up to a tablespoon per plant of blood meal, or twice that amount of cottonseed meal, for example. First, wet the soil a day of so prior to application, then scatter the fertilizer around the root areas and scratch it into the soil. Thoroughly water in the fertilizer. Mulches of

. . . *Roses (continued)*

compost, manure, or sludge will supply additional nutrients.

Although the list of pests and diseases which *can* bother roses is long, most gardeners will have to contend with only a few of the potential problems. First-line defense is garden sanitation; removal of dead leaves and old mulch at pruning time—coupled with a dormant lime-sulfur or oil spray—will eliminate eggs and breeding places of insects and destroy over-wintering spores of blackspot and rust.

For the problems that do occur during the season, see pages 44-51 (including the chart on page 50) for methods and materials to combat them. Another means of avoiding pest problems is to plant your roses in a mixed bed among various other plants: Insects that favor roses won't live as freely in a mixed border as they will in a mass planting that contains only roses.

EVERGREEN SHRUBS AND TREES

These are garden mainstays in warm-weather regions, generally, and especially in the Pacific coast states, the South, and the Mid-Atlantic region. As winter temperatures go lower—either due to altitude or latitude—the selection of broad-leafed plants declines. The first step, therefore, is to know your area's climate and the climate of your particular garden. In cold-winter climates a knowing gardener often can succeed with plants considered somewhat tender for his area by selecting consistently warmer or protected sites for these plants. Locations that are sheltered from winter winds or from early-morning sun favor plants whose leaves would be fatally desiccated or whose frozen tissues would be too-quickly thawed, respectively. Locations which will always be warmer than the coldest temperature readings are: against walls of buildings especially under an overhang), a southern exposure, sloping land, land near oceans or other large bodies of water. Because these plants retain all (or a part) of their leaves throughout the year, they can be moved and planted only with soil around their roots. For general planting directions, see "Planting balled-and-burlapped plants or plants from containers" on page 27. If it is necessary to stake the plant, do this while you are planting it so that you can be sure the stake won't damage roots when it is inserted.

Generally, broad-leafed shrubs and trees are pruned only to guide their shape or—in the case of hedges—to control their growth to a particular form or area. Watering, then, is the only routine maintenance job, and here again the various plants differ in their preferences. Depending upon your climate, some broad-leafed evergreen plants may require some winter protection.

With such a diverse assortment of plants represented in this category, only a generalization is possible for fertilizing recommendations. Immediately before (or just as) a plant starts a growth cycle is the time to give a light application of organic nitrogen. A mulch of compost should supply enough of the other nutrients and some nitrogen as well. Some plants (notably most herbs) prefer no fertilization.

Conifers

Pines, spruces, fir, and their relatives are the only evergreen trees or shrubs possible in many of the cold-winter regions. Tolerance to cold does vary from species to species—so does acceptance of mild winters. Select kinds that will succeed in your climate. All are sold balled-and-burlapped or as container-grown plants. For general planting instructions, see page 27. Most conifers need a well-drained soil.

Even though the needle- or scale-like leaves offer little surface to the drying winter wind, it is sometimes advisable to provide a temporary winter wind screen of burlap or other tough material between the plant and the prevailing wind; this will prevent desiccation and consequent "burn" which results when transpiration through leaves is faster than roots can take in moisture from frozen or cold soil. Also in winter, be sure to shake snow off conifer branches; the weight of it can cause limbs to break off.

Usually no fertilizing is necessary.

Acid-loving plants

Some familiar garden plants (such as rhododendrons, azaleas, many heathers, camellias, blueberries) thrive in a slightly to strongly acid soil. But in much of the Southwest, and generally where rainfall is low, soils and water tend to be alkaline.

The alkalinity problem is this: as soil *pH* increases (see page 18), certain nutrients (especially iron) necessary for growth of acid-loving plants become unavailable; plants then become chlorotic (leaves turn yellow but veins remain green), lose their vitality, and soon die. In low rainfall areas, alkaline salts accumulate in the soil and damage roots; burned leaf edges indicate salts damage.

Your county agricultural extension service can tell you if your soil is acid, neutral, or alkaline and whether its alkalinity (if that is the case) is from excess calcium, sodium, or both. Soil sulfur is effective on high-calcium alkaline soil; dig it into soil in early spring—warmth and moisture slowly make sulfur available to counteract alkalinity. One pound per 100 square feet lowers *pH* one-half point. Use gypsum in high-sodium soil to get rid of the sodium, then add sulfur to increase acidity.

Prepare the soil for these plants with acid reacting organic materials—such as peat moss or redwood products. Many acid-loving plants demand good soil aeration, and alkaline soils tend to be very compact. Where water is alkaline, periodically flood the soil to leach salts from the root zone. If drainage is poor, grow these plants in raised beds.

General directions for preparing the soil in an annual bed are on page 23. Once the soil is prepared, you have a choice of two methods for raising annuals: planting seedlings from flats, or sowing seeds in the area in which they are to remain. First, however, select annuals that will do well in your climate. Nasturtiums, for example, grow well in cool climates, but zinnias prefer heat.

You can raise your own annuals from seed (see page 29) or set out plants from a nursery. In either case, timing is important: Most seedlings, if put into cold, wet soil will just stand still until soil warms up. The same advice applies when you sow seed in the open ground.

In frost-free areas, open ground seeding can take place in fall or early spring. April and May are best in areas that have definitely cold winters. First, rake smooth your prepared soil, breaking up or removing all clods and discarding rocks. You can then broadcast the seed or plant it in rows; in either case, cover the seed to the depth indicated on the seed packet (generally about twice the diameter of a seed) with the prepared soil or screened compost. Orient the rows to take advantage of the sun's path; a north-south direction will give equal sunlight on both sides of the row. Soak the seedbed with a fine mist of water, and repeat watering as often as is necessary to keep the surface moist (a very thin mulch or strips of burlap over the seeded area will help conserve moisture).

After seeds germinate you may need to protect seedlings from birds by placing a wire or plastic mesh over them; bait for snails or slugs if they are a problem. After two pairs of true leaves develop, thin crowded plants by removal or transplanting. If you live in a cool-summer area, follow spacing directions on the packet. In hot climates, close planting is a good idea; the plants' leaves will shade the soil, thus helping to keep roots cool and moist.

If you set out plants from flats, the transplanting operation will be the most critical process. Prepare the soil as for a seedbed (see above) and water soil well at least a day before you intend to put out plants. Cloudy or foggy days are ideal for setting out plants. Early morning is preferable; next best time is the late afternoon, for the plants then have the night hours in which to recover from the shock of transplanting. This is especially helpful to plants with large leaf surfaces such as zinnias, petunias, or marigolds.

To remove plants from flats, first be sure soil is moist (but not so wet that it will pack into a mudball). Rather than cut plants out of a flat, try to lift a corner of the mass of plants and gently pull each and its soil away from the others. Dig generous-sized planting holes and set plants in holes slightly lower than they were in the flat (except for stock—plant it slightly high). Fill in around the root ball with soil, leave a shallow basin around the plant, and water thoroughly. Mulch after watering to conserve water, inhibit weed

growth, prevent soil caking and water runoff. If the weather is hot, shade the plants from direct sun for a few days with cardboard or shingles; or burlap, newspapers, or wrapping paper supported on stakes.

Water annual plantings deeply and repeat whenever the top inch or two of soil dries out (here, again, a mulch helps out); a vigorous, leafy plant will help shade its own roots. Overhead watering will be satisfactory until plants begin to bloom; then, try to flood irrigate whenever possible—especially with the taller growing sorts which might fall over if watered from above.

There is a point in each annual plant's development when tissues harden, growth stops, and the seed part of the growth cycle is triggered; anything you can do to prevent premature hardening of the plants will prolong bloom. Tissues harden if the supply of nutrients gives out before the plant is mature; cold nights or hot weather have the same effect; so do drying winds. Lack of water and damage to the plant by disease or insects also contribute to this. Always keep faded blooms picked off (to prevent seed formation); this can encourage more flowers to form even after hardening has begun.

Annuals—like vegetables—should be kept actively growing. About 14 days after germination, begin fertilizing with a liquid nitrogen fertilizer such as fish emulsion or blood meal mixed 1 tablespoon to a gallon of water. Keep this up every two weeks until flower buds form.

PERENNIALS

The first consideration in any perennial planting is selection of the planting site. Most perennials prefer, if not require, sun—and good drainage is essential. Where drainage is poor, the easiest solution is to plant in raised beds or containers. Especially for the taller growing kinds (like delphinium) a location which will not be exposed to strong winds is desirable. Avoid planting near shallow-rooted shrubbery which will compete with the perennials for moisture and nutrients. Basic soil preparation directions appear on page 25.

After you select a congenial planting site, the next step is to *plan* the garden. If you want an area devoted primarily to perennials or with a mixture of perennials and annuals, be sure that the different plants you choose have the same soil moisture, and climate preferences. Peonies, for example, prefer a heavy rich soil, while yarrow (Achillea) wants lighter, drier soil. Beyond this, the selection of various plants involves artistic decisions. As you plan the location of your perennials, think of the color and texture associations—both of flowers and of foliage. Because different perennials bloom in different seasons, you will have to decide whether you want a planting which will provide a glorious display for about a month or whether you prefer one which will flower for several months but with less concentrated mass color. By spacing the spring, summer, and fall blooming plants throughout one

planting you can maintain a colorful, interesting garden spot for most of a year's flowering season.

Prime maintenance requirement of a perennial planting is water; a mulch (see page 30) will help conserve moisture and also keep down the weed population. As they come into bloom, some perennials will require staking to keep their flowers off the ground; this includes tall growing types like delphiniums and hollyhocks, and those with heavy flower clusters or sprawling growth such as gypsophila or veronica.

Although perennial implies permanence, most plants under this classification need to be periodically dug, divided, and replanted. Frequency varies according to kind: Chrysanthemums are best if replanted or started from cuttings each year; iris need replanting every 3-4 years; peonies and Oriental poppies—which resent disturb-

ance—may remain much longer. Proper time to dig and divide varies according to the particular perennial; often it is in the month or two following flowering.

Fertilizing begins with preparation of the soil (see page 20) at which time you should incorporate generous amounts of coarser grades (which last longer) of phosphorus and potassium fertilizers; bone meal and rock phosphate are two good sources, respectively. In the years that follow, fertilize plantings in spring when growth is starting and again in early summer. For the spring fertilizing, work bone meal into the soil around plants to about a 2-inch depth and also apply an organic nitrogen fertilizer. In summer, give plants only a light organic nitrogen application. Whenever you replant any portion of a perennial bed, be sure to incorporate phosphorus and potassium fertilizers into the soil to the depth that you expect roots to penetrate.

BULBS

General directions for preparing soil that is to receive bulbs appears on page 25. Deep digging is a good practice, but let this be your guide: Most bulbs are planted 3 times as deep as their greatest diameter, and their roots will go down twice as deep (or more) as the depth of the bulb itself.

The ideal soil for most bulbs is one that is porous and drains well but holds water for the roots. If your soil is heavy clay and drains slowly, or very sandy and does not hold water, make sure you incorporate a 3-4-inch layer of organic material to a depth of about 12 inches in the area where you intend to plant your bulbs.

If you will plant a large number of bulbs in one bed, it is often easier to excavate the entire area to the proper planting depth, work the phosphorus and potassium fertilizers into the sunken area you have just created, place the bulbs, and cover them all at one time. If

you plan to combine bulbs and annuals or perennials in the same area, it is generally best to set out the surface plants first, then plant the bulbs; then there will be no danger of planting directly on top of the bulbs. But if it's more convenient to reverse the procedure, mark the position of each bulb; even weeks later you will be able to plant the surface plants without fear of super-imposing them on the bulbs hidden in the ground below.

Water bulbs thoroughly at planting time to provide moisture they need for active root growth. Usually this watering will be sufficient until the tops of the plants appear. Continue watering, after bulbs have finished blooming, until leaves naturally turn yellow. Never cut leaves off while they are still green, as the green leaves provide nourishment which is stored in the bulb for the development of next year's bloom. If you need to dig bulbs before foliage has matured, lift them carefully—so as to disturb

roots as little as possible—and heel them into the ground where they can continue growing and ripening their leaves. The best digging tool is a spading fork; you can slice through a bulb easily with a spade.

In hot dry climates, mulches are extremely helpful in keeping soil cool during warm weather following bulb planting. In cold-winter areas, mulches of straw, salt hay, evergreen boughs, pine needles, or non-packing leaves are useful in preventing alternate freezing and thawing of the soil which can heave bulbs and damage the less-hardy kinds (such as the bulbous irises).

Insects which may bother bulb plants are aphids, mites, and thrips. See the chart on page 50 for possible controls.

Bone meal and a rock potash mixed into the bulb's root-zone soil at planting time should provide enough nutrients for the life of the bulb planting.

How to Grow Lawns

Lawn grasses fall into two categories. The cool-season grasses withstand winter cold but languish in hot, dry summers; this group includes bent, fescue, bluegrass, rye, and redtop. They are grown in the Northeast through Midwest to the Northwest, and to an increasingly lesser extent as you progress South and Southwest. The subtropical grasses, on the other hand, flourish in summer heat but perish in cold Northern winters; these consist of the Bermudas, zoysias, and St. Augustine grass. In addition, dichondra—which is not a grass—is used as a lawn, primarily in the Southwest.

There are three methods for lawn planting: seeding, sodding, and planting stolons or plugs. For seeding, the planting season is spring through fall. Spring seeding gives grass a long growing season in which to get established, but summer heat and weed growth may require extra maintenance effort. Fall sowing reduces the danger of heat injury and rampant weed growth, but it must be done when you can expect at least 6 weeks of 50° to 70° weather for the grass to get a good start before heavy frosts come and soils turn cold. See page 28 for how to prepare soil for planting a lawn. When soil is ready, pick a windless day to evenly broadcast the grass seed—or distribute it with a mechanical spreader. Rake in the seed very lightly to insure contact with the seedbed. If you expect hot or dry weather, mulch the seedbed with a 1/8-3/16-inch layer of moistened peat moss, aged sawdust, or finely screened compost. After mulching, roll with an empty roller. Keep soil dark with moisture until all grass has germinated.

If you plant a lawn from sod strips, prepare soil as though you were going to sow seeds but work for a surface about 3/4-inch lower than the finished level you desire. Unroll the sod on the prepared soil and lay the strips side by side with all edges touching; stagger the ends of the sod strips as in a bricklayer's running bond pattern. After all sod strips are in place, roll the sod with a 1/2-full roller to smooth out rough spots and bond the sod with the soil. Watering more carefully than normal is necessary only for a few days. Aside from sodding, the only way to get a lawn of the grasses which produce no seeds (such as hybrid Bermudas and zoysias) is to plant plugs or stolons of these grasses. Soil preparation is the same as for making a seedbed (see page 28). If you plant from stolons, the simplest method is to broadcast them over your prepared soil at the rate of 3-5 bushels for every 1,000 square feet, then roll the planting with a 1/2-filled roller. Mulch the area with a 1/2-inch layer of screened topsoil, moistened peat moss, aged sawdust, or screened compost. Roll again after applying the mulch, then water the area. Thereafter, water the mulched surface frequently (maybe several times a day in warm weather) so it will not dry out at any time. Another method for planting stolons begins with pre-soaking the prepared planting area a day or so in advance. Then, while soil is still moist but dry enough to work without sticking, make a series of parallel trenches about 2 inches wide, 3 inches deep, and 10 inches apart. Plant individual stolons in trenches so that when trenches are filled in the green grass blades will be above soil grade level and all of the white parts will be below. Water the area soon after planting, and keep it moist continually until the stolons have rooted and begun to grow.

The two primary maintenance requirements of all lawns are watering and mowing. For best appearance (and lawn health) regular mowing is a must; once a week is generally satisfactory. If you live in a region of naturally acid or alkaline soil, you should check your lawn soil's pH every year or two. Whenever you discover that pH has gone below 6 or over 8, check with your county agricultural extension service for recommendations, for soil in your area, to bring pH back to neutral. Ground limestone is the usual remedy for soils too acid; cottonseed meal and acid organic materials used as a topdressing (most wood products, for example) will generally counteract alkalinity. The subtropical grasses that grow from stolons should have an annual thatch removal in late winter or early spring. A rake manufactured for this purpose makes the job easy for small to medium sized lawns; a mechanized thatch remover is available for large lawn areas. See page 52 for a discussion of some common lawn pests.

Nitrogen is the principal nutrient required by lawns for healthy, green growth. Because of differences in soils and climates, your lawn's need for nitrogen may differ from that of a lawn in a neighboring county, but the color and vigor of the grass can show you the nitrogen need. After your eye becomes trained, you can tell well-fertilized grass from nutrient-starved grass by noting the shade of green. Easier than that, you tell the need by the number of times per month or per week the lawn needs cutting. If you find you can let more and more days go by between mowings—first, from 5 days to 8 days, then from 8 days to 14 days—you need to put on more fertilizer. (One exception, however, is that bluegrass needs autumn fertilizing despite naturally limited growth at that time.) The University of California recommends 1 pound of actual nitrogen (see page 15) per 1000 square feet per month—when grass is growing, not during the months when ground is frozen or grass is naturally dormant. If your idea of the correct timing does not coincide with this, you can make your own adjustments in amount to apply at each fertilizing.

Index

PHOTOGRAPHERS

GLENN CHRISTIANSEN: 28, 46 (bottom right). LYN DAVIS: 38. RICHARD DAWSON: 33 (bottom). RICHARD FISH: 33 (top). LES FLOWERS, JR.: 47 (bottom center). ART HUPY: 47 (top right). WILLIAM MARKEN: 30 (left). ELLS MARUGG: 5 (right), 12 (all), 13 (all), 27 (bottom right), 52 (center). GRACE M. MILLER: 47 (bottom left). DON NORMARK: 31, 39 (top left), 41 (all), 45, 47 (top left and center, bottom right), 54. PETER REDPATH: 22 (bottom), 27 (bottom left). DARROW WATT: cover, 5 (left), 21, 22 (top), 25 (all), 27 (top), 29 (all), 30 (right), 32, 35 (all), 39 (top right, bottom), 42, 46 (top, bottom left and center), 49 (all), 51, 53 (all). HERMAN J. WILLIS: 52 (left and right).